You Can't Do It All:
Effective Delegation
for Supervisors

By Jeanne Baer

American Media Publi
4900 University Avenue
West Des Moines, Iowa 50266-6769 U.S.A.
800/262-2557
www.ammedia.com

You Can't Do It All:
Effective Delegation for Supervisors

Jeanne Baer
Copyright© 1999 by American Media, Inc.

Credits:
American Media Publishing: Art Bauer
Todd McDonald
Editor in Chief: Karen Massetti Miller
Designer: Scott Rhone
Cover Design: Maura Rombalski

Published by American Media, Inc.
4900 University Avenue
West Des Moines, IA 50266-6769

Library of Congress Catalog Card Number 98-74673
Baer, Jeanne
You Can't Do It All: Effective Delegation for Supervisors

ISBN 1-884926-99-1

Printed in the United States of America
01 00 99 98   9 8 7 6 5 4 3 2 1

Introduction

Most accomplished leaders would agree that delegation is one of the most important skills (if not *the* most important skill) in their repertoire.

Why? Imagine your own situation: Are you a manager or supervisor who comes in early, stays late, and gives 110 percent? Then delegation will help you improve your results while decreasing the time you spend at work.

Do you wish your employees were more loyal to you or the organization? When you delegate well, your employees widen their horizons, develop new skills, and enjoy a new level of authority. That usually leads to an impressive increase in loyalty and commitment.

Would you like to move up? As you use your newly freed time to tackle tougher organizational issues, you'll become a more valuable contributor—and highly promotable!

In short, effective delegation produces a win all around!

It's much more difficult to *practice* effective delegation than it is simply to *understand* it. But if you apply this book's techniques, you'll find yourself managing the delegation process with assurance in no time!

About the Author

As the founder of Creative Training Solutions, Jeanne Baer designs and delivers training programs to create more effective, productive teams and individuals. A performance improvement consultant to organizations across the U.S. and in Europe, she is also a frequent presenter at state and national conferences.

Jeanne's work has been published by McGraw-Hill, Pfeiffer and Company, Jossey-Bass/Pfeiffer, and Harvard Business School Publishing. Her "Managing Smart" column appears monthly in *Strictly Business* magazine and elsewhere. Active in the American Society for Training and Development since 1987, Jeanne currently serves as a National Advisor to Chapters. She was president of the Lincoln, Nebraska, ASTD chapter in 1993.

Jeanne received her bachelor's degree from the University of Nebraska and has done graduate work in accelerated learning principles at Colorado State University. She serves on the adjunct faculty of two colleges in Lincoln, Nebraska.

● Table of Contents

Chapter *One*

Delegation: Barriers, Busters, and Benefits

Chapter Objectives

▶ Define what delegation is and what it isn't.

▶ Identify 12 barriers to effective delegation and 12 barrier busters.

▶ Recognize the ways delegation can benefit supervisors, employees, customers, and the entire organization.

Whitney looked at the clock on her desk and sighed. Everyone else had gone home hours ago, but if she left now, she'd never get caught up. "I knew being a supervisor would be a challenge, but if I'd known it would take this many hours, I would have run the other way when they offered that promotion," Whitney said to herself as she sorted through yet another pile of papers. "Maybe I'm just not supervisor material. None of the other supervisors seem to be staying this late. I wonder what they're doing that I'm not?"

Defining Delegation

> "It takes a deep commitment to change and an even deeper commitment to grow."
> —*Ralph Ellison*

If you're a conscientious manager or supervisor in today's workplace, chances are you often arrive at work early and stay late. In that case, someone has probably told you, "You should delegate more—leverage your productivity!"

And if you've struggled with delegation, you're not alone. Although the ability to delegate is extremely important to your overall success as a manager or supervisor, it's also one of the most difficult skills to master.

Finally, if you've been the victim of an unskilled attempt at delegation, you know what delegation isn't: It *isn't* assigning people "grunt work"—boring, meaningless tasks. Nor is it giving people jobs that don't allow any room for initiative or growth. Nor is it a situation in which a manager abdicates responsibility, assigning a task with no guidance or follow-up.

So what is delegation?

Delegation is:

◆ Assigning a whole unit of work (a task from start to finish) to an employee who is capable of doing it.

◆ Giving that employee authority for the final completion of that work.

When a manager or supervisor delegates well, he or she also:

◆ Discusses the task in advance with the employee to be sure the task fits into the employee's current schedule.

◆ Allows the employee to achieve goals in her or his own way.

◆ Trains and/or guides the employee when the need arises.

As empowering as good delegation sounds, delegators must keep in mind that they are still *ultimately responsible* for the outcome of the job. They can delegate authority, but not responsibility!

Riding a Tandem Bicycle

One way to think of delegation is to compare it to riding a tandem bicycle. Like a tandem bike, delegation requires two active participants to make it work—the delegator and the delegatee. And like the riders on a tandem bike, each has a different role to play.

When a delegation is done well, the delegator places the delegatee in the front seat of the tandem. That means the delegatee is responsible for setting the pace and steering. But this doesn't mean the delegator can get off the bike. Just as the second rider must support the first by pedaling and steering in the same direction, the delegator must provide the delegatee

1

Delegation is assigning a whole unit of work to an employee who is capable of doing it.

with the resources, encouragement, and—if appropriate—advice he or she needs to complete the assignment. Together, both riders move the bike—and the delegation—toward its goal.

Identifying Barriers to Delegation

Many people never learn to delegate because they're too busy thinking about why they *can't* delegate! As you read the following list, put a check mark in front of each statement you have also used as a reason for not delegating.

❑ I hate dumping jobs on people who are already too busy.

❑ My boss might think I'm lazy—that I'm not doing anything.

❑ My employees would just gripe and be mad at me if I gave them more to do.

❑ I'm more of a "doer" than a delegator, and I like doing these things. I'm not sure I'd have such a sense of achievement doing new, unfamiliar work instead.

❑ Doing it myself gives me a high profile, and I like the recognition.

❑ My boss told me to do this task.

❑ I can do the job better than anyone else—I have the most experience.

❑ It's just a habit—I do it almost before I realize it.

❑ I don't know my employees well enough to know who could do other jobs.

❑ There's no time to delegate. We need results quickly, so it's easier to do the task myself.

❑ If I delegate too much and people develop key skills, my own job might be in jeopardy.

❑ My employees don't have the information I have to make decisions.

Many people never learn to delegate because they're too busy thinking about why they can't delegate!

Take a Moment

Review the statements that you marked as your reasons for not delegating. Are they really valid? Can you find flaws in the logic? Use the space below to jot down some arguments against them.

Hint: Think of the possible benefits to yourself, your organization, and your employee(s) if and when you *do* delegate well.

_____

_____

_____

Breaking Down the Barriers

As you reviewed the previous list of reasons for not delegating, something might have become apparent to you—they aren't valid reasons at all! They are excuses—excuses that create barriers to delegation.

When you let these barriers keep you from delegating, you shortchange yourself and your employees. But you can overcome these barriers. Let's consider a set of responses to the excuses we just encountered. By thinking through all 12 responses, you'll be armed with a full arsenal of barrier busters to break through any old habitual excuses that are getting in the way of your success!

> **When you let these barriers keep you from delegating, you shortchange yourself and your employees.**

◆ **I hate dumping jobs on people who are already too busy.**
Then don't dump! Good delegating means assessing your employees' current workload, deciding what might be eliminated, streamlined, or reassigned, and then assigning something new. Besides, aren't you awfully busy, too? Have some consideration for your own workload!

◆ **My boss might think I'm lazy—that I'm not doing anything.**
You'll impress your boss more by delegating than doing! Your boss probably realizes that it takes more time and skill to train someone than to do a familiar I-could-do-this-in-my-sleep job yourself.

9

◆ **My employees would just gripe and be mad at me if I gave them more to do.**
Again, you'll want to pave the way by assessing your employees' current workloads. Try to give them *better* work rather than just *more* work, and explain how the delegated tasks will help them grow professionally. One more thing: If your employees can control you by simply griping a bit, who's supervising whom? Just say "no" to manipulation.

◆ **I'm more of a doer than a delegator, and I like doing these things. I'm not sure I'd have such a sense of achievement doing new, unfamiliar work.**
But you didn't have that sense of achievement when you first began that job, did you? Then your fear of the unknown may have made you dread that job as much as you're dreading your current one. Once you've gotten comfortable with these higher-level skills, you'll have the same sense of satisfaction and contribution.

◆ **Doing it myself gives me a high profile, and I like the recognition.**
Then double it! If you can train someone else and later report a successful result, both you and your employee will shine. Also, if you like doing a task, chances are your chosen employee will, too. Therefore delegating something you could keep for yourself builds loyalty and motivation among your staff.

◆ **My boss told me to do this task.**
Chances are, your boss just wants the task done well, and she or he doesn't care how or by whom. You're expected to accomplish things through others. You increase your value as a supervisor when you develop the skills of your employees.

◆ **I can do the job better than anyone else—I have the most experience.**
Probably true! But you and your employees will never enjoy the considerable benefits of good delegation if you don't allow them to practice and develop their own skills. Give them some solid on-the-job training and observant feedback. Know that even with your good coaching, their productivity will dip until they master a new task. Then their productivity will rise dramatically, and you can put your energy elsewhere.

◆ **It's just a habit—I do it almost before I realize it.**
As the saying observes, old habits die hard. Instead of mindlessly reacting and doing a task the next time it pops up, be proactive. Make a plan now and begin training someone else to do it.

◆ **I don't know my employees well enough to know who could do other jobs.**
Get to know them! You can observe your employees at work, talk to them about their strengths and goals, and/or give them the chance to try small projects on their own. When an employee shines, you'll know that person is capable of more. The tips in later chapters of this book will help you match the right employee to the task.

◆ **There's no time to delegate. We need results quickly, so it's easier to do the task myself.**
This approach makes sense if you're referring to a once-a-decade task. But if it's a job that comes around routinely, taking the time to train and coach an employee now will save you much more time in the long run.

◆ **If I delegate too much and people develop key skills, my own job might be in jeopardy.**
But if you don't delegate, your value as a manager or supervisor is limited, which puts you in higher jeopardy! Besides, some experts say the best way to be promoted is to train your replacement—that way, you can be freed to take a new position without a loss in productivity.

> **If you don't delegate, your value as a manager or supervisor is limited.**

◆ **My employees don't have the information I have to make decisions.**
Information is power, and everyone needs as much information as possible to effectively solve problems and make wise decisions. When company policy allows, provide employees with the information they need to make sense of a delegated task. When company policy dictates that you should *not* share a specific type of information with employees, delegation may not be an option, and you will have to do the job yourself.

Reasons or Excuses?

By generating ideas about barrier busting, you can begin to change your attitude about delegating.

By now, you may have realized that some of your reasons for not delegating were actually *excuses*—attitudinal barriers that kept you from developing your full potential as a manager or supervisor. You may also have realized that by generating ideas about barrier busting, you can begin to change your attitude about delegating. The following exercise offers one more tool that will encourage you to learn and practice effective delegation skills.

Take a Moment

On a day-to-day basis, how do you feel about your workload, and how do you handle it? Check those statements below that represent how you feel or behave.

❑ I'm always checking up on my people to make sure they're doing their assigned tasks properly.

❑ I work under constant pressure. When I'm on vacation or out sick, I worry about what's happening at work. I'm too tired to do much with my friends or family when I'm not at work.

❑ I get so bogged down in the details of the jobs below me, I don't have enough time for training, organizing, or planning.

❑ Every day, I'm interrupted by crises I have to handle, decisions employees want me to make, or questions they need me to answer about how to do their work. I don't have time to do my own work.

❑ Some of my employees are always asking me for additional assignments or responsibility.

❑ I don't have any qualified subordinates who could replace me if I were promoted.

If you checked even *one* of the above items, you should know that life will be different once you master the skills of effective delegating. You'll free up time, cut down stress, and be a more likely candidate for promotion!

Sharing the Benefits of Effective Delegation

Although this book is designed to maximize the benefits of delegation for you, keep in mind that delegation also benefits others.

Benefits for Employees

◆ **Improved morale**
Employees chosen for delegation usually feel respected, appreciated, and trusted. When they succeed at a new assignment, they feel a sense of accomplishment.

◆ **Enhanced skills**
As a result of learning new skills, employees are often more valuable and more promotable.

◆ **Enhanced job responsibilities**
Learning a new skill or taking over a project allows employees to add some variety to a repetitive workload. (This can be especially valuable when there's little opportunity for upward movement.)

Take a Moment

Can you think of other benefits delegation may have for your employees?

_____

_____

_____

Benefits to the Organization

◆ **Improved task/pay fit**
If you're doing jobs that people who get paid less could be doing, then it makes sense for them to do it rather than you.

◆ **Increased work contribution**
When you delegate well, you can spend newly freed time to solve higher-level problems, create big-picture strategies, and develop or enhance your own skills.

◆ **Increased talent development**
When you delegate, it stretches you and the delegatee. And when the delegation is successful, the company benefits from your abilities as a coach and the employee's abilities as a key player who may have supervisory potential in the future.

◆ **Improved productivity**
As employees' morale and skills get a boost, productivity rises and turnover falls. Often, both the delegator and the delegatee want to learn and contribute more as a result of their positive experience with a successful delegation.

◆ **Increased innovation**
When a different person takes on a task, chances for innovation increase. A fresh perspective may help your organization find ways to save considerable amounts of money, time, or effort.

Take a Moment

Can you think of other benefits delegation can have for your organization?

_____

_____

_____

1

Benefits to Customers

◆ **Improved efficiency**
When supervisors try to do too many different tasks, they're often not very skilled at any. When employees are encouraged to master something new, they often become quite good at it, providing excellent service to the customer (and at a lower cost, in terms of their salary or wages).

◆ **Increased accessibility**
When customers need attention, but only the supervisor (you) has the needed information, the result is delays and impatience. Your organization will not appreciate your being the information bottleneck.

◆ **Improved consistency**
If you're the only one working with customers, chances are you rely on your own common sense, but you haven't standardized any procedures for providing service in the most effective, efficient way. On the other hand, if you share knowledge and responsibility with an employee, you're likely to formalize your best practices. As a result, everyone doing that job can adopt them, and good service is guaranteed, no matter who provides it.

Take a Moment
Can you think of other benefits delegation can have for your internal or external customers?

Chapter Summary

In this era of flattened organizations, where supervisors and managers have a wider span of control, the ability to delegate effectively is more important than ever. However, it's also one of the hardest managerial skills to master.

Managers and supervisors avoid delegating for many reasons: They may believe they don't have time, or they may be afraid their employees won't do the task properly. They may even worry that their employees will do a task better than they've been doing it themselves!

However, each of these reasons is actually only an excuse to procrastinate. Once managers and supervisors do invest the time and effort to delegate properly, they find that they have more time, less stress, and more marketability.

Meanwhile, employees experience a boost in both their morale and their skills while the organization enjoys increased productivity and a more versatile, committed workforce.

As you can see, although effective delegating is difficult, it's a skill well worth learning!

Self-Check: Chapter One Review

Answers to the following questions appear on page 114.

1

1. Which of the following is not delegation?
   a. Abdicating responsibility for a task
   b. Assigning a whole unit of work to an employee who is capable of doing it
   c. Giving an employee authority for the completion of a task
   d. None of the above

2. True or False?
   When a supervisor delegates a task, she or he must provide employees with step-by-step instructions rather than letting them try to achieve goals in their own way.

3. Which of the following is a valid reason for not delegating?
   a. I hate dumping jobs on people who are too busy.
   b. There's no time to delegate. We need results quickly, so it's easier to do the task myself.
   c. Because of company policy, I can't provide employees with the information they need to effectively solve problems and make decisions.
   d. All of the above.

4. True or False?
   If you can train someone else to do a task, you increase your own opportunities for promotion.

5. Who is ultimately responsible for the outcome of a delegated task?

   _____

Chapter *Two*

Finding Time and Tasks to Delegate

Chapter Objectives

▶ Identify your own time-waster activities.

▶ List the tasks that make up your job and how much time you spend doing them.

▶ Name five times when you should delegate.

▶ Name three times when you shouldn't delegate.

After one too many late nights at the office, Whitney realized that the only way she could keep up with all of her responsibilities was to delegate more. She decided to talk to Pat, a veteran manager at her company who was known as an excellent delegator.

"I want to delegate right," Whitney said when the two met in Pat's office. "But it seems that I can't even find the time to plan the delegation, much less carry it out!"

"Well, as an up-and-coming manager, you'll be expected to spend more and more of your time on key tasks that contribute directly to the achievement of goals—on activities that yield big results," Pat observed. "But too often, we develop some bad habits that eat up hours of time every day. You may be spinning your wheels on time wasters—trivial things that get you nowhere! Let's take a look at how you spend your day."

> **"Managers often spend so much time trying to do things right, they rarely get around to doing the right things."**
> *—Peter Drucker*

Eliminating Time Wasters

As a manager or supervisor, you need to invest your time in two important areas:

◆ Priority activities related to organizational goals

◆ Developing your employees

However, many supervisors find that lower priority activities eat up their time so that they are unable to accomplish these important responsibilities. Fortunately, you can control and conquer many of these time wasters. The following list contains some of the most common ways supervisors and managers waste time. As you read through the list, put a check beside those you would like to banish from your life.

Common Time Wasters

❏ Procrastinating—putting things off—because of fear, dread, or confusion

❏ Shuffling papers instead of filing them, tossing them, or taking action

❏ Taking overextended lunches and coffee breaks

❏ Allowing constant interruptions from others (or yourself!)

❏ Backtracking due to forgetfulness

❏ Not using "prime time" (when your energy is high) for priority work

❏ Worrying instead of resolving a problem or issue

❏ Communicating unclearly, which results in confusion, resentment, mistakes, and other problems

❏ Not actively listening, which causes the same time-consuming problems as unclear communication causes

❏ Maintaining perfectionist standards—taking too much time to finish a task in order to make it perfect

❏ Filing too much and throwing away too little so that eventually it takes too long to find anything

2

Many supervisors find that lower priority activities eat up their time so that they are unable to accomplish more important responsibilities.

❑ Being unable to make a decision, which causes a ripple effect of delays for several people, processes, or functions

❑ Writing ineffectively so that too much time is spent rewriting

❑ Reacting to crises as they arise instead of planning and taking the action steps that accomplish goals

❑ Searching for misplaced items

❑ Not having self-imposed deadlines so that you allow tasks to remain unfinished

❑ Not having facts or phone numbers on hand

❑ Allowing upward delegation (taking on jobs from those who work for you or offering to check into or handle a matter of interest to them)

❑ Writing instead of phoning

❑ Doing other people's work

❑ Checking and answering voice mail and e-mail more often than necessary

❑ Subscribing to and dealing with electronic mailing lists and other Internet services that overwhelm you with interesting but inessential information

Take a Moment

As you read through the above list, did other bad habits occur to you? If so, list them below:

_____

_____

_____

How many time wasters do you need to eliminate? Keep this list handy, and resolve to eliminate as many of these bad habits as possible! (For additional help with time management issues, see *Investing Time for Maximum Return* and *How to Get Everything Done (And Still Have a Life)*, both published by American Media, Inc.)

Is It Necessary?

Some time wasters may be disguised as seemingly useful activities. Try to avoid spending time on activities such as:

❑ Writing reports that are no longer needed.

❑ Attending meetings that don't require your input.

❑ Following procedures that no longer match your job.

❑ Generating correspondence that serves no useful purpose.

❑ Generating correspondence that is routed to more people than need to see it.

2

Take a Moment

Are you currently spending time on other activities that are no longer useful? List them below. Then consider how you can eliminate these useless activities or change them so that they help you accomplish your key goals.

_____

_____

_____

Choosing Tasks to Delegate

■ "Okay, I can see I have some room for improvement when it comes to managing my time," Whitney confessed. "So what comes next? Do I just call everybody into my office and say 'Who wants to do what?'"

"No, good delegating is much more complex than that," Pat replied. "You need to thoroughly analyze your own job and the tasks you perform before you even begin to think about assigning them to other people."

Once you've eliminated your time wasters and taken control of how you spend your workday, the next step in the delegation process is to break down your job into all of its components, listing every activity. Though this is a time-consuming task, think of it as an important investment in your future. Knowing exactly what you do will help you match the right tasks to the right employees, which will mean less work for you in the long run.

To analyze your activities more carefully, you may wish to use the following Job Breakdown Worksheet. The worksheet asks you to list each activity you do, the amount of time you spend doing it, and the reason why you are currently doing it yourself.

Do you know why estimating the time spent on each activity is important? It will give you insight into three important facts:

◆ What a task costs the company when you do it

◆ How much time you'll be able to free up when you delegate that task

◆ How much time someone else will have to free up in order to take over that task from you

You also need to consider why you are currently doing each task—especially the recurring ones—yourself. Is it because it's good for your ego? Is it a key activity that can only be done by someone at your level? Does it give you visibility or recognition? If you don't have a good reason why you must do a job, then it's time to delegate it.

Job Breakdown Worksheet

Tasks I perform on a regular basis	Time spent monthly	Reason(s) I must do them
1.		
2.		
3.		
4.		
5.		
6.		
7.		
8.		
9.		
10.		

Take a Moment

Fill out the Job Breakdown Worksheet. List as many of your usual tasks as you can think of—use extra paper if necessary. In order to realize how much you actually do, you may wish to list everything you can think of now and then return to your list in several days and add to it. Add to it again in a week or two.

Don't worry yet about which tasks should be delegated—we'll consider that in our next exercise.

When Should You Delegate?

As you prepared your Job Breakdown Worksheet, you probably identified several tasks that you could delegate. To help you hone your list further, consider these five situations—they're all excellent opportunities to delegate.

- **Delegate when the activity doesn't make the most of your abilities but *does* make the best of someone else's.**
  Are you a "task person," terrific at getting things done but not as accomplished when it comes to working with people? Then perhaps you could delegate attending a meeting, helping customers, or serving on a task force to one of your employees. On the other hand, if you're more of a "people person," perhaps one of your employees would be better than you are at taking inventory or doing another task where accuracy is paramount.

  You can also delegate when specialized knowledge is needed and someone else has more of it than you do. Perhaps your field has become quite complicated, and you have difficulty keeping up on a certain issue. Is there someone who has expertise in that area or who is quite interested in it?

- **Delegate when the payoff is low.**
  This payoff might be a personal one, but first and foremost, it means a company payoff. Consider any activities that are simply trivial, day-to-day activities rather than key tasks. Remember, as a supervisor or manager, you should focus on strategic planning, directing, and other managerial tasks that will help your company succeed.

- **Delegate when the job is repetitive.**
  This is an excellent opportunity to delegate. The payoff for your time investment is high because once you've trained an employee to do this task, time is freed up for you every time he or she does it. Although spending 15 to 20 minutes a day on a repetitive task may not seem like much, it quickly adds up to a major block of time better spent elsewhere.

  Remember, your repetitive duties may seem like drudgery to you, but they may be novel and interesting to someone else. For instance, perhaps travel has lost all its spark for you but

> As a supervisor or manager, you should focus on strategic planning, directing, and other managerial tasks that will help your company succeed.

might be a real perk for one of your employees. Or perhaps scheduling employees' work hours is a complex, time-consuming job to you but might be an interesting challenge to someone else, and it would give that person a broader perspective on how your whole operation works.

● **Delegate when you have much more expertise than the activity needs.**
Many of the jobs you do probably don't require your level of ability and experience. Perhaps it's time to give another person a chance; after all, those jobs would be new and interesting to someone else.

● **Delegate when you need to develop your employees.**
In some cases, you may be doing activities others could do simply because you enjoy them. But delegating in order to develop your employees is smart for three important reasons:

• Giving your employees interesting things to do will help them stay motivated.

> Giving your employees interesting things to do will help them stay motivated.

• Delegating a fun task shows employees that you care about them. It's easy to tell people you care about them, but this demonstrates it convincingly.

• When you give your employees opportunities to build their skills, you're readying replacements for the time when you want a promotion. After all, no one will allow you to move up if your department will be a shambles without you!

Knowing When Not to Delegate

Before you've assigned every possible task to one of your employees, be aware that there are three situations in which you should never delegate:

● **Never delegate the responsibility for disciplining an employee.**
For both practical and ethical reasons, a reprimand or termination should always come from the manager or supervisor.

◆ **Never delegate praising an employee.**
It's enjoyable to give positive feedback, and it forms a bond between you and your employees. It also means more to employees when the praise comes from you than when it comes from someone else. In fact, employees may even resent it if they work especially hard and you think so little of their dedication that you send someone else to toss them a compliment.

◆ **Never delegate when a situation is confidential.**
What's confidential? Any time a situation involves personnel records, such as disciplinary action, salaries, or medical information. Examples also include tasks involving proprietary information, trade secrets, certain customer data, or security data—all these tasks should remain with you.

Take a Moment

Return to the Job Breakdown Worksheet you completed in the previous exercise. Which of your activities fall into one of the following categories?

1. Activities that don't make the most of your abilities but might make the best of someone else's, or activities that require a specialized knowledge: Can you think of a case where someone's personality or expertise might be more suited to a task than yours is?

2. Activities for which the payoff is low: Do you have a low-payoff job that should be done by someone else?

3. Activities that are repetitive: Can you think of any repetitive duties that might seem interesting to someone else?

4. Activities that don't need your high level of expertise: What are some tasks for which you're *over*-skilled?

5. Activities that, though fun for you, would develop your employees: What are some tasks that would be good developmental opportunities for your employees?

Chapter Summary

Often, supervisors and managers want to delegate, but because they never find the time to delegate right, they never get around to it at all. Therefore, your first task on the road to effective delegation is to identify those activities that are eating up your time without giving you much in return. Once you've identified and banished some of your time wasters, you can use your newly acquired time to continue with the steps of delegating.

Next, you will choose which task(s) to delegate. You begin by listing all the tasks that make up your job and how much time you spend doing them. Then ask yourself why you are currently doing each task. Could a task be done by someone else, or must it be done only by you? Using a Job Breakdown Worksheet will reveal additional valuable information by pushing you to analyze your activities and attitudes more carefully.

Finally, you'll want to remind yourself of the five situations that present excellent opportunities to delegate and three situations that you should *not* delegate.

2

Self-Check: Chapter Two Review

Answers for these questions appear on pages 114.

1. What are the two most important areas in which supervisors need to invest their time?

   a. _____

   b. _____

2. Which of the following is not a time waster?
   a. Maintaining perfectionist standards
   b. Estimating the amount of time you spend on each job activity
   c. Allowing upward delegation
   d. All of the above

3. List five situations that provide excellent opportunities to delegate.

   _____

   _____

   _____

   _____

   _____

4. List three situations in which you should never delegate.

   _____

   _____

   _____

5. True or False?
   When determining which tasks to delegate, it's a good idea to delegate those tasks that don't make the most of your abilities but to keep those tasks you enjoy doing even though someone else could do them.

Notes

2

Chapter *Three*

Matching the Employee to the Task

"❝I never really thought before about how many things I do each day," Whitney said as she looked up from her Job Breakdown Worksheet. "No wonder I can't get everything done! But now that I understand what I do, how do I start giving it away?"

"Before you can give tasks away, you have to understand the people you want to give them to," Pat said. "Not everyone has the right qualities to succeed at every task. Let's take some time now to talk about your employees."

> **"Presence is more than just being there."**
> —*Malcolm S. Forbes*

Now that you've identified some tasks you believe can be delegated, the next step is to match those tasks to the most appropriate employees. If the task in question is a small one, choosing an employee to complete it may be easy. But if it's large, you'll improve your chances of success by considering two important factors:

◆ What personality characteristics are necessary to complete this task?

◆ What abilities are needed in order to complete it?

Identifying Personality Characteristics

Do you know your employees well enough to match their personal qualities with those needed for a task? You can begin to identify your employees' *personality characteristics* by paying attention to how they do their jobs and what they're interested in. What motivates your employees to do their best? What are their suggestions and complaints? When you know your people well, you can bring out their best—and that allows your best to shine, too.

Introverts or Extroverts?

3

One important personality characteristic that can influence whether a person is suited to a job is whether that person is an introvert or an extrovert. *Introverts* are comfortable working by themselves and can concentrate on individual tasks for long periods of time. *Extroverts,* on the other hand, prefer working with others as either a team member or a team leader.

Introverts are comfortable working by themselves. *Extroverts* prefer working with others as a team member or team leader.

People Oriented or Task Oriented?

Another important personality characteristic to consider is whether an employee is people oriented or task oriented. *People-oriented* employees strive to maintain good interpersonal relationships and will sometimes put this goal ahead of meeting a deadline or following a specific procedure.

Task-oriented employees are more concerned with facts than with feelings. They are sometimes willing to sacrifice relationships in order to complete a task by deadline and up to standard.

People-oriented employees strive to maintain good relationships. *Task-oriented* employees may sacrifice relationships to complete a task.

Combining the Characteristics

These four personality characteristics—introvert, extrovert, people oriented, and task oriented—work together to create a variety of *personality traits.* They combine in the following ways:

- ◆ Introvert/People oriented
- ◆ Introvert/Task oriented

- ◆ Extrovert/People oriented
- ◆ Extrovert/Task oriented

We can get a closer look at the combined personality characteristics and the traits they create by placing them in a grid format:

Personality Grid

Extrovert

People Focused	Task Focused
Outgoing	Very Direct
Sees "Big Picture"	Dependable
Poised	Organized
Persuasive	Quick Decision Maker
Good Interpersonal Skills	Self-Starter
Open	Practical
Individualistic	Forceful

People Focused - **Task Focused**

Patient	Calm
Empathetic	Good Analyzer
Team Player	Thorough
Helpful	Has High Standards
Trusting	Meticulous
Accessible	Factual
Loyal	Unemotional

Introvert

The form on the following page uses the Personality Grid to analyze the characteristics required for a task you would like to delegate. *Before you fill out the form, you may wish to photocopy it so you'll have blank copies for future use.*

Take a Moment

Use the form on the following page to analyze a task that you have been thinking of delegating. When you have determined what personality characteristics are needed to perform the task, ask yourself which of your employees have those characteristics.

What Personality Traits Are Needed?

Description of Task: _____

_____

Consider the following personality traits. Put a +++ by the traits that are essential to the performance of this task. Put a ++ by those that would be very useful. Put a + by those qualities that would be nice to have. Leave those you don't need for this task blank.

Extrovert

People Focused	Task Focused
__ Outgoing	__ Very Direct
__ Sees "Big Picture"	__ Dependable
__ Poised	__ Organized
__ Persuasive	__ Quick Decision Maker
__ Good Interpersonal Skills	__ Self-Starter
__ Open	__ Practical
__ Individualistic	__ Forceful

People Focused ----------------------------- **Task Focused**

__ Patient	__ Calm
__ Empathetic	__ Good Analyzer
__ Team Player	__ Thorough
__ Helpful	__ Has High Standards
__ Trusting	__ Meticulous
__ Accessible	__ Factual
__ Loyal	__ Unemotional

Introvert

Now list the employee(s) you have who possess one or more of these characteristics and the characteristics they possess:

1. _____

2. _____

3. _____

4. _____

5. _____

Identifying Necessary Abilities

Of course, personality characteristics aren't the only factors that determine whether an employee can successfully complete a task. Many tasks also require special abilities, such as familiarity with a particular type of computer software, in-depth knowledge of your products or services, or the ability to speak a foreign language.

The list of abilities a delegatee might need is as varied as the number of tasks you might have to delegate. Here are just a few to consider and the types of tasks that might require them:

Abilities	Type of Task
Physical strength	Heavy lifting or moving
Physical coordination	Product assembly
Mechanical skills	Taking things apart and putting them back together
Math skills	Keeping a budget, balancing books, or tracking product performance
Computer skills	Using various software programs
Equipment skills	Running various pieces of equipment
Writing skills	Writing reports, memos, or other documents
Public-speaking skills	Making formal presentations
Interpersonal skills	Dealing with people one on one
Foreign-language skills	Communicating with speakers of other languages
Telephone skills	Dealing with the public over the phone
Critical-thinking/problem-solving skills	Analyzing data and developing solutions
Creative-thinking skills	Developing new programs or product ideas
Product or service knowledge	Working with customers or vendors
Knowledge of organization's policies	Dealing with procedural or human resource issues
Knowledge of organization's politics	Making proposals or presentations

How does this all work? Suppose you decided to delegate preparing the monthly sales report to one of your employees. You might look for someone with good math skills for preparing the sales figures, good critical-thinking skills for analyzing the figures, and good writing skills for preparing a report based on the figures. If you wanted the person to use spreadsheet and word-processing software to prepare the report, you would also look for specific computer skills.

The following form sums up the abilities we have just discussed. You can use it to help you analyze the skills required for a task you would like to delegate. *Before you fill out the form, you may wish to photocopy it so you'll have blank copies for future use.*

What Abilities Are Needed?

Description of Task: _____

_____

Consider the following abilities. Put a +++ by the abilities that are essential to the performance of this task. Put a ++ by those that would be very useful. Put a + by those abilities that would be nice to have. Leave those you don't need for this task blank.

Abilities
____ Physical strength
____ Physical coordination
____ Mechanical skills
____ Math skills
____ Computer skills (Type of software: _____)
____ Equipment skills (Type of equipment: _____)
____ Writing skills
____ Public-speaking skills
____ Interpersonal skills
____ Foreign-language skills
____ Telephone skills
____ Critical-thinking/problem-solving skills
____ Creative-thinking skills
____ Product or service knowledge
____ Knowledge of organization's policies
____ Knowledge of organization's politics

Other important abilities:

1. _____

2. _____

3. _____

Now list the employee(s) you have who possess one or more of these abilities.

1. _____

2. _____

3. _____

4. _____

5. _____

3

Putting It All Together

Once you've determined the personality characteristics and abilities needed for a task, the next step is to bring all of the information together into a matrix and rate your potential delegatees. The matrix prompts you to consider a few other important factors—questions to ask about the candidates. If necessary, you can use these questions as tiebreakers. Altogether, this instrument will allow you to come to a sound conclusion.

The following case study demonstrates how to create a matrix and rate your candidates. At the end of the case study is a blank matrix form for your own use.

Case Study: Whitney's Choice

■ Whitney wanted to delegate the task of resolving customer complaints. She had three employees she believed were potential candidates for the task.

Step 1: Identify Necessary Characteristics and Skills
Whitney began by determining what personality characteristics and skills were necessary to complete the task. She used the Personality Characteristics and Abilities forms presented previously to determine which of these qualities were most important:

Necessary personality characteristics:

◆ Empathy

◆ Patience

Necessary skills and abilities:

◆ Problem-solving skills

◆ Knowledge of organizational policy

- ◆ Interpersonal skills

- ◆ Creative-thinking skills

- ◆ Telephone skills

Step 2: Fill Out the Matrix Form

Next Whitney used the qualities she identified in Step 1 to fill out the matrix form. She put the most important personality characteristics and skills (those that received three plus signs on the rating forms) at the top of her list.

Step 3: Rate the Employees

The next step is to rate the characteristics and skills of the employees under consideration. You can create a ranking system based on the number of employees you are considering. For example, if you're comparing two employees, give the person who is better in an area two points and the other person one point. If you're considering four employees, give the best person four points, the next best person three points, and so on. Here's how Whitney rated her employees:

> You can create a ranking system based on the number of employees you are considering.

3

Task/Employee Match-Up

Task: Helping customers solve problems (resolving complaints)

Employees Under Consideration:

Characteristics and Abilities Needed	LaShea	Toni	Lee
1. Empathy	1	3	2
2. Problem-solving skills	3	2	1
3. Policies knowledge	3	2	1
4. Communication skills	1	2	3
5. Creative-thinking skills	1	2	3
6. Telephone skills	1	2	3
7. Patience	1	3	2
Total Number of Points	11	16	15

■ Based on her matrix, Whitney could see that Toni scored the most points. "So Toni gets the assignment, right?" Whitney asked Pat. "Actually, I think I instinctively knew she was the one without doing all this."

"Well, some people don't know that without going through the process," Pat replied. "Besides, if you take time to analyze documentation in this way, you'll have a record in case an employee wants to discuss why you chose whom you did for a task.

"But don't make your decision quite yet," Pat continued. "It's a fairly close race. That's why you should consider a few additional factors.

Step 4: Consider Other Factors

After you rate potential delegatees on the matrix, ask yourself the following questions about your candidate(s):

1. How much time do you think this task will take? Which candidate(s) has/have the time available to do the task?

2. If an otherwise good candidate lacks some skills, can she or he acquire these skills quickly enough to do the job?

3. Who is the most reliable?

4. Who is the most interested in additional responsibility?

5. Who is your first choice to do this task?

6. Who is your backup choice?

■ "Uh oh!" sighed Whitney when she read the first question. "Now that I think about it, Toni has less time than anyone to take on something new!"

She went on to the second question. "Who can acquire necessary skills? Because Lee is new, he isn't as confident about our policies as the other two are. But I'm sure he could master our problem-solving model—he just needs some practice.

"Third—who's the most reliable? Not a problem—all of them are.

"Fourth—who wants additional responsibility? Well, I've got to admit I've been so busy doing all the work, I haven't talked to anyone about that! So I'll have to do that. But for now, at any rate, I think I'm most comfortable delegating this task to Lee, especially when he's up to speed on policies and our problem-solving method."

Though it had taken some time, Whitney was pleased with the results of her delegation. "You know, Pat, this really works!" she said at the end of their session. "It's given me an actual system instead of a haphazard guess. Thanks for your help."

3

Take a Moment

Use the following matrix form to determine the results of your own delegation.

Before you fill out the following form, you may wish to photocopy it so you have blank copies for future use.

Task/Employee Match-Up

Task: _____

Ratings: Write the appropriate number on the line corresponding with each employee and the particular characteristic/ability. Use 1 as your lowest rating.

Names of Employees Under Consideration:

_____   _____   _____

Characteristics and Abilities Needed (prioritized):

1. _____   _____   _____   _____

2. _____   _____   _____   _____

3. _____   _____   _____   _____

4. _____   _____   _____   _____

5. _____   _____   _____   _____

6. _____   _____   _____   _____

7. _____   _____   _____   _____

8. _____   _____   _____   _____

9. _____   _____   _____   _____

10. _____   _____   _____   _____

_____

Total Number of Points   _____   _____   _____

Passing Tasks Around

■ "There's one more thing to keep in mind," Pat said as Whitney was about to leave. "Be sure you pass your delegation around—don't give all your tasks to one person, even if that person does seem to have the time."

There are at least three reasons for *not* giving all of your delegation assignments to one employee:

◆ It's not fair to the "honoree." This employee might be reluctant to admit it but might feel quite overburdened with "opportunity."

3

◆ It could create hard feelings among employees—a singled-out employee might be the object of peer-group pressure.

◆ It's not fair to your other employees. Even though they may be a little slower to learn or take more of your time to coach, they deserve the opportunity to build their skills as much as your superachiever does.

Giving all your delegated tasks to one person isn't fair to the delegatee and could create resentment among other employees.

As you can see, though choosing the best candidate for a delegation assignment can take some time, the results will be much more reliable than simply picking an employee who has some free time. By following a logical system for task assignment, you can delegate your tasks to the employees who have the best chance of completing them successfully.

Chapter Summary

Once you've identified some delegatable tasks, you need to match those tasks to the most appropriate employee(s). Using an organized system will improve your chances of success.

First, identify what personality characteristics and abilities are needed. Second, determine which employees have those qualities. If you don't know your candidate(s) for the task fairly well, observe how your employees do their jobs, what they're interested in, and what suggestions and/or complaints they have. (When you know your people well, you can bring out their best, and that allows your best to shine, too.)

Once you've compared your employees' personality characteristics and abilities with what's essential to succeed at the task, the natural choice may be readily apparent. However, before making a final choice, you'll also want to consider the following:

- ◆ Which candidate(s) has/have the time available to do the task?

- ◆ If an otherwise good candidate lacks some skills, can s/he acquire these skills quickly enough to do the job?

- ◆ Which person is the most reliable?

- ◆ Which is the most interested in additional responsibility?

And last but not least, as tempting as it may be to delegate repeatedly to a proven "winner," be fair—make it a point to spread your assignments around.

Self-Check: Chapter Three Review

Answers for these questions appear on page 115.

1. Match the personality characteristics with their descriptions:

___ People who match this personality type enjoy meeting the public, working in teams, making speeches, and persuading others.

___ These people are more concerned with facts than with feelings. They are thorough, analytical, and meticulous.

___ These people are helpful, patient, empathetic, and loyal to their fellow employees and to the organization. They are team players who strive to maintain good relationships.

___ People who match this personality type enjoy working by themselves, pay careful attention to detail, and are capable of concentrating on individual tasks for long periods of time.

    a. Introverts
    b. Extroverts
    c. People-oriented employees
    d. Task-oriented employees

2. If you wanted to delegate a bookkeeping task that required use of a spreadsheet program, what abilities would you look for?
    a. Physical coordination
    b. Computer software skills
    c. Public speaking skills
    d. Math skills
    e. b and d
    f. All of the above

3. True or False?
If a candidate has the personality characteristics and abilities necessary to do a task, you should delegate the task to that person regardless of his or her current schedule.

4. True or False?
Delegating all of your tasks to one employee could create resentment among other employees.

3

Chapter *Four*

Preparing for the Delegation Meeting

Chapter Objectives

▶ List three reasons why it's important to prepare carefully for delegation.

▶ Consider and decide how you will respond to 10 delegation issues before meeting with the delegatee.

▶ Explain why interim checkpoints are important, and name three variables that will help you determine how frequently they're needed.

"**T**ed—come in! Sit down! I'll tell you why I called you in. You know, I've been observing you, and I think you're very bright."

"Well, thanks, Martina! I like working here, and . . ."

"That's why I've selected you for an important opportunity that will give you both a challenge and increased visibility!"

"Well, thanks for your confidence! I hope I'm up to . . ."

"No problem! I'm leaving for vacation tomorrow. I'll be gone for two weeks, and I'm leaving you completely in charge of the store."

"What? But . . . um . . . well . . . how will I know . . ."

"Oh, don't look so worried! If something comes up that you don't understand, just take a good guess! I know you'll do a great job. Well, that's all. Thanks for coming in to talk about it."

"Talk? Oh . . . uh, yeah. Right."

"Never launch a vast project with a half-vast plan."
—*Kay Borden*

If you've ever been on the receiving end of a conversation like the previous one, you know how bewildered or even panic-stricken the delegatee feels! Use this example as a reminder to thoroughly explain the assignment when you begin to delegate.

The example is also a reminder of the obvious—that it's not enough to toss the job to an unprepared employee and then abdicate, hoping for the best. Following a system for communicating the delegation will help you remember all the important steps, ensuring a successful delegation each and every time.

> **Thoroughly explain the assignment when you begin to delegate.**

4

Take a Moment

You need to consider 10 important issues whenever you're planning a delegation. Can you guess what they are? Recall your own past experience as a delegator or a delegatee, and fill in the blanks that follow by choosing a word from those at the end of the exercise. Once you've finished, turn to the next page to verify your answers. (Note: You won't need five of the available words.)

1. Consider how you will describe this _____ to the delegatee.

2. Consider what you might say to help the employee _____ this delegation.

3. Consider the employee's present _____.

4. Consider what additional _____ the employee might need to perform the task well.

5. Set clear _____ for the task you've selected.

6. Consider the _____ (if any) on how the job should be done.

7. Consider any nasty _____ that could crop up.

8. Consider how much _____ the delegatee will have.

continued on the next page

Take a Moment (continued)

9. Determine the project's deadlines and also when you'll
_____ the completed project with the delegatee.

10. Establish interim _____ so you can make
sure the person is making progress.

Word Choices

checkpoints	motivation	energize	constraints	goals
assignment	authority	welcome	success	review
priorities	training	workload	surprises	solutions

Making the Assignment: Ten Issues

An important part of any successful delegation is being prepared
for your meeting with the delegatee. One way you can do that is
to consider 10 important issues that can affect the success of the
delegation. How many were you able to identify in the previous
exercise? Here are descriptions of all 10.

1. **Consider how you will describe this *assignment* to the
delegatee.**
Help your delegatee understand both the details of
completing the task and how it fits into the big picture:

- What is the purpose of the task?

- How does it relate to the goals of your area or your
organization?

- How has the task been done in the past (if it has)?

- Why are you delegating it now? Be honest: Is it to free up
your own time, or do you really expect this assignment to
be an interesting stretch for the employee? Don't destroy
your credibility by insisting that a "sow's ear" is a "silk
purse." Note: Employees may be more accepting of
mundane assignments if they understand how the
assignments relate to the goals of your area and the
organization.

- When will the assignment begin?

- Do you welcome changes/improvements in how it's done?

2. **Consider what you might say to help the employee** *welcome* **this delegation.**

   Goals are met by employees who choose to meet them, not by employees who are *ordered* to meet them. By understanding some of the things that motivate your employees and then explaining to them how doing this job relates to their interests, you'll get stronger commitment to the assignment.

   • Why did you choose her or him, and why are you confident she or he can do it?

   • What previous experience will serve the employee well in this situation?

   • How might taking this assignment benefit the employee —what's "in it" for him or her? Will it mean more visibility? Skill building? A break from the routine? A new challenge? In short, how might the "payoff" fit with the employee's career goals?

   4

3. **Consider the employee's present** *workload.*

   Never ask an employee to "do it in your spare time." This type of delegation:

   Never ask an employee to "do it in your spare time."

   • Implies that you believe the employee isn't always busy and has spare time that is currently wasted.

   • Means the job will probably never get done, due to confusion over its importance or because of conflicts with other tasks the delegatee must do by a certain date.

   • Trivializes the job. If the assignment isn't important enough to make time for, why do it at all?

   Work with the delegatee to determine how you might reprioritize or reassign some of the delegatee's tasks to allow her or him to succeed at this one.

4. **Consider what additional** *training* **the employee might need to perform the task well.**

   Can the employee get up to speed quickly enough?

Quantify the results you want as specifically as possible.

5. **Set clear *goals* for the task you've selected.**
   Quantify the results you want as specifically as possible. What will success look like? How will results be measured and performance be evaluated?

6. **Consider the *constraints* (if any) on how the job should be done.**
   If you specify as few constraints as possible, you'll find your employee will:

   - Be more motivated and committed to the job because she or he gets to call the shots.

   - Feel free to be innovative or make improvements in past methods.

   - Derive optimum learning, whether s/he succeeds or fails.

7. **Consider any nasty *surprises* that could crop up.**

   - What unusual circumstances or "danger points" should the delegatee know about? What could possibly go wrong, or has gone wrong in the past?

   - How can that be avoided?

   - What should the employee do if it occurs—come to you to discuss possible solutions? Take action and report to you what she or he has done?

8. **Consider how much *authority* the delegatee will have.**
   Remember, your employee is accountable to you, but you are accountable, in the end, for the accomplishment of this task.

   - What resources will she or he control? What tools, equipment, and dollars will be available?

   - Do you need to take steps to make any resources available?

   - Will there be any new reporting relationships or lines of communication associated with this assignment?

   - Whom else will he or she work with or interview?

- Do you need to clear the way for your delegatee by talking or writing to these people?

- What types of decisions may she or he make, and which ones should be made by you or someone else?

- Under what circumstances do you want to review or approve the delegatee's work? For instance, if the delegatee is to design a plan of action, is he or she to get your approval before proceeding? Or design it and simply inform you? Or design it and use it without your seeing it?

9. **Determine the project's *deadlines* and a date when you'll *review* the completed project with the delegatee.**
The review date should be far enough ahead of the final deadline that the employee (or you, in an emergency) could take corrective action if necessary. And remember, since the delegatee will need more time to do the job than you would, she or he should start earlier than you would.

4

10. **Establish interim *checkpoints* so you can make sure the person is making progress.**
The frequency of these checkpoints will depend on how complex the job is, how many people are involved, and how experienced the delegatee is.

Take a Moment

Use the following worksheet to help you plan your own upcoming delegation meeting. In some cases, you won't be able to make a final decision about an issue without talking to the delegatee. Nevertheless, you should have a pretty good idea about these issues when you begin your meeting.

Before you fill out the worksheet, you may wish to photocopy it so you'll have clean copies for future use.

Delegation Issues Worksheet

Task: _____

Delegatee: _____

1. How will you describe this assignment to the delegatee?

   • What is the purpose of the task?

   _____

   • How does it relate to the goals of your area or your organization?

   _____

   • How has the job been done in the past (if it has)?

   _____

   • Why are you delegating it now?

   _____

   • When will the assignment begin?

   _____

   • Do you welcome changes/improvements in how it's done?

   _____

2. What can you say to help the employee welcome this delegation?

   • Why did you choose him/her, and why are you
     confident s/he can do it?

   _____

continued on the next page

Delegation Issues Worksheet (continued)

- What previous experience will serve the employee well in this situation?

  _____

- How might taking this assignment benefit the employee—what's "in it" for him or her? How might the "payoff" fit with the employee's career goals?

  _____

3. How might you reprioritize the employee's present workload or reassign some of the delegatee's tasks to allow him/her to succeed at this one?

   _____

4. What additional training will the employee need to perform the task well? Can the employee get "up to speed" quickly enough?

   _____

5. What are your goals for the task you've selected? Quantify the results you want as specifically as possible.

   _____

6. What are the constraints (if any) on how the job should be done? (Specify as few constraints as possible.)

   _____

7. What nasty surprises could crop up?

   - What could possibly go wrong or has gone wrong in the past?

     _____

continued on the next page

4

Delegation Issues Worksheet (continued)

- How can that be avoided?

  _____

- What should the employee do if it occurs—come to you to discuss possible solutions? Take action and report to you what she or he has done?

  _____

8. How much authority should the delegatee have?
   (Your employee is accountable to you, but you are accountable, in the end, for the accomplishment of this task.)

   - What resources will she or he control? What tools, equipment, and dollars will be available?

     _____

   - Do you need to take steps to make any resources available?

     _____

   - Will there be any new reporting relationships or lines of communication associated with this assignment?

     _____

   - Whom else will the delegatee work with or interview?

     _____

   - Do you need to clear the way for your delegatee by talking or writing to these people?

     _____

continued on the next page

Delegation Issues Worksheet (continued)

- What types of decisions may the delegatee make, and which ones should be made by you or someone else?

  _____

- Under what circumstances do you want to review or approve the delegatee's work?

  _____

9. What is the project's final deadline? What is a date ahead of that deadline when you'll review the completed project with the delegatee?

   _____

4

10. Establish interim checkpoints so you can make sure the person is making progress. At what points in the assignment do you want to review progress on this delegation?

    _____

Benefiting from Preparation

Do you think these preparatory steps will take a lot of time and energy? You're right, they will! But taking time now will save a great deal of time and stress for both you and your delegatee later:

- You'll both be clear about expectations.

- The delegatee will have all the information she or he needs to start out with confidence.

- You'll create a consistent method for delegating instead of a haphazard approach that yields unpredictable results.

And if those three reasons aren't enough, here's a fourth—you'll also serve as a role model for your employees when they delegate to others!

Take a Moment

Let's read the minds of a few delegators who didn't consider some preparatory issues. Read each statement and then glance through the list of delegation issues on pages 46 to 49. After each statement, write down the number of the issue(s) you think they skipped and what the delegator should have done instead.

Answers appear on pages 115–116.

1. "Now Bill says he doesn't understand the program! I had no idea! Why didn't he tell me that weeks ago, when he could have attended training?"

   Issue #_____

   What the delegator should have done:

   _____

2. "Julia was blindsided. She says she had no idea that Shipping would dig in their heels and resist her implementation of the new plan. I thought everyone knew the people in Shipping would need some persuading. But now, they're so mad they're not even speaking to us!"

   Issue #_____

   What the delegator should have done:

   _____

3. "What was Sherm thinking?! He allocated the funds without even checking with me, and now we're stuck with his decision. I'll never delegate anything again!"

   Issue #_____

   What the delegator should have done:

   _____

continued on the next page

Take a Moment *(continued)*

4. "I really thought Huong Le would write up a more thorough analysis than she did. When I asked her about it, she said she'd had two other high-priority projects competing for her time. I wish I'd known about the other projects sooner."

Issue #_____

What the delegator should have done:

_____

5. "Oh, man. I thought Jacob was a lot further along than this. The deadline is tomorrow, and he's hardly started! I guess he didn't realize exactly when it was due. This is really going to look bad for me at the meeting."

Issue #_____

What the delegator should have done:

_____

4

Chapter Summary

After selecting an assignment and the best employee to carry it out, you'll meet with that employee and delegate the responsibility. But before the meeting, carefully consider 10 important issues involving the assignment, its goals and deadlines, and the amount of authority the delegatee will have.

By thinking these issues through in advance, and by being prepared to discuss them with the delegatee, you'll set the employee up for success. Not only will you prevent misunderstandings, you'll also save yourself and the delegatee time, energy, and stress as he or she works through the assignment.

Self-Check: Chapter Four Review

Answers to these questions appear on page 116.

1. Name three reasons why it's beneficial to prepare carefully before meeting with the delegatee.

    a. _____

    b. _____

    c. _____

2. You need to delegate a task in order to free up some time. You know it's not going to be fun or even much of a "stretch" for the delegatee. Why should you be honest about your purpose instead of enthusiastically building up the assignment?

    _____

3. Why should you plan to review the completed project with the delegatee a day or more ahead of when it's actually due?

    _____

4. Why should you build in some interim checkpoints?

    _____

5. The frequency of these checkpoints depends on what three variables?

    a. _____

    b. _____

    c. _____

Notes

4

Chapter *Five*

Conducting the Delegation Meeting

Chapter Objectives

▶ Recognize the importance of two-way communication during the delegation meeting.

▶ Recognize various types of nonverbal feedback that indicate delegatee concerns.

▶ Ask questions that will help you get straightforward verbal feedback from delegatees.

▶ Agree on the delegatee's level of authority.

Whitney had thought long and hard about her first delegation. She analyzed her work to identify a good, delegatable task; she carefully selected just the right employee to assume responsibility for it; and she thoroughly considered the 10 important delegation issues. She was prepared! Here's what she said during her first delegation meeting:

"Thanks for coming in, Lee. I've got an important job, and I know you're the perfect person for it. I've observed what motivates you, so I know you're going to enjoy it and learn a lot from it. By the looks of your personnel file, you've done similar work, so I don't think you'll need training.

"You'll have access to any information you need. The deadline is a month from today, and I'll meet with you once a week to check your progress. I've taken the liberty of reassigning a couple of your jobs to Lou for the next month. Well, let's get started!"

Remember in Chapter One when we compared delegation to pedaling a tandem bicycle? That partnership begins here in the delegation meeting as the delegator and the delegatee develop a

> "Empowerment comes from teaching others things they can do to become less dependent on you."
> —*Ken Blanchard*

shared understanding about expectations for the assignment. To ensure their ride ends safely at the desired destination, they should explore all issues related to the delegation through open, two-way communication. By the end of the delegation meeting, the delegator should be confident that the delegatee fully understands what the task involves and accepts the assignment. In our opening example, Whitney had no way of knowing if Lee understood or accepted the assignment because she never gave Lee a chance to talk!

Take a Moment

Return to the Delegation Issues Worksheet in the previous chapter. The last time you delegated a task, which of these issues did you consider and discuss with your delegatee?

_____

_____

In the future, what will you do differently at your delegation meetings?

_____

_____

5

Ensuring Understanding

Shared understanding is important because misunderstanding is so expensive! How expensive is it? Take your hourly wages or salary times the number of hours you spent preparing for the delegation meeting. Then add the value of the time both you and the delegatee spend in the meeting. Then, once miscommunication causes problems, add in the value of the time spent correcting them. To that sum, add a large portion of resentment, frustration, confusion, disappointment—all of those emotions that drain an organization of its vitality and productivity.

You can avoid this waste of time and money by taking the time *now* to be sure you and your delegatee understand each other. One of the best ways to do this is to ask for *feedback*, or reactions,

One of the best ways to make sure you and your delegatee understand each other is to ask for feedback.

from your delegatee and to actively listen to her or his responses. As you speak with your delegatee, keep in mind that feedback can take many forms. It may be nonverbal, relying on facial expression or body language. Or it may be verbal, taking the form of a comment or question.

Take a Moment

Imagine that you're explaining something to someone, and you're watching for nonverbal feedback that will tell you how your message is being received.

1. What are some signs that the person understands or agrees with your message?

   _____

   _____

2. What are some signs that she or he is confused or worried?

   _____

   _____

3. What are some signs that he or she understands but doesn't agree or doesn't want the assignment?

   _____

   _____

Responding to Feedback

Your goal in your delegation meetings is to encourage employees to express themselves openly, ask questions when they don't understand, and express concerns when they think they will have difficulty completing a task. Some employees will feel comfortable providing you with this feedback with little prompting. Others may be more reluctant to ask questions or express concerns. Perhaps they are afraid of appearing "stupid" in front of the boss, or perhaps they do not want to be perceived as having a negative attitude.

As the previous exercise suggests, people can express agreement, confusion, or disagreement in a variety of ways that do not involve words at all. As you talk with your employees, look for facial expressions and body language that express confusion, hesitancy, or disagreement. These could include the following:

◆ Frowning

◆ Head shaking

◆ Lack of eye contact

◆ Sitting with arms folded across the chest

◆ Nervous laughter

◆ Hesitancy to answer

You should also listen for noncommital statements like "I guess so" or "If you think so."

If you pick up signs that a delegatee seems confused or hesitant, don't ignore them or try to gloss over them. Remember, the delegatee must fully understand and accept the assignment in order for the delegation to succeed. A misunderstanding now could mean failure later. Ask questions, and encourage your delegatee to provide you with honest feedback.

As you ask your questions, don't try to engineer the response you want from the delegatee. Avoid questions like "You don't think you'll have any problems, do you?" or "I think this will be right up your alley, don't you?" or "You're not afraid of a little extra work, are you?" Your delegatee will certainly see these "helpful" questions for what they are—loaded and manipulative.

Instead of asking leading questions like these, try to find out what your delegatee really thinks. Ask *open-ended questions*— questions that require more than a yes-or-no-answer—and engage in a candid dialogue about your delegatee's concerns.

> As you talk with your employees, look for facial expressions and body language that express confusion, hesitancy, or disagreement.

5

Common Concerns

Delegatees may express a variety of concerns during the delegation meeting. Three common areas of concern are:

◆ Confusion regarding the task.

◆ Lack of experience.

◆ Disagreement with the assignment.

Here are some ways that delegators can respond to each.

Resolving Confusion

■ "So that's that task as I see it," Fred said to his employee Danielle. "Got any questions?"

"Uh, no, I guess not," Danielle said hesitantly, but her frown told Fred she really didn't understand.

When faced with a confused look, delegators often ask, "Did you have a question?" Or they'll finish what they think is a tidy explanation with, "Got any questions?" But many delegatees are reluctant to admit that they don't understand, so they just say no.

One way to be sure a delegatee understands an assignment is to ask that person to paraphrase what you've just said.

One way to be sure a delegatee understands an assignment is to ask that person to paraphrase what you've just said. When you make this type of request, be sure to do it in a supportive way rather than making it seem like a test:

■ "Just to be sure we're on the same page, let's review what you're going to be doing on the project. What's your understanding of the first step?"

■ "Let's go over the process one more time just to be sure I explained it thoroughly. How would you begin?"

Going over the assignment in this way gives the delegator and the delegatee the chance to engage in further dialogue without forcing the delegatee to openly state, "I don't understand."

Dealing with Lack of Experience

Some delegatees worry that they don't have the experience or expertise to do the job well. When they express these concerns, some delegators respond by blurting out something like, "Oh, don't worry—if I can do this, anyone can!" This is a mistake for several reasons:

◆ It implies that the task is trivial—certainly too trivial to worry about.

◆ It implies that the delegator really doesn't want to address any fears the delegatee might have.

◆ It implies that the delegator is unskilled, clumsy, or inadequate in some way.

◆ It implies that the delegatee is just as inept as the delegator!

If your delegatee doubts his or her ability to do the task, return to the reasons you believe she or he can do it and talk about training possibilities. You can describe some of your own experiences when you first did the task:

■ "You know, I was pretty worried the first time I did this job, too. But I found that if I took it one step at a time, it wasn't nearly so intimidating."

■ "After the first couple of times I did this job, I found I was really improving my speed. So don't worry if it's a stretch at first—it's supposed to be. And I won't expect you to do it as fast as I do it until January."

■ "I'll be here if you get stuck—not to take the job back, but to explore options with you."

Handling Disagreements

When you get subtle signs that your delegatee disagrees with what you're saying or doesn't want the assignment, don't ignore the signals! You may be tempted to hope that the delegatee will come to accept the assignment over time, but sweeping problems under the rug now means failure later. Besides, by encouraging your delegatee to be honest, you may discover that the objections are based in a simple misunderstanding that you can easily clarify.

5

> If your delegatee doubts his or her ability to do the task, return to the reasons you believe she or he can do it.

To help the delegatee be open, tell him or her what you're observing and encourage a response. Here are some examples:

■ "Nick, you looked uncomfortable when I said you'd be working with Sid. How do you feel about that aspect of the job?"

■ "What's wrong, Jesse? From the way you're rolling your eyes, I know that something is! Tell me about it."

■ "When I said I'd like to approve your plan, Carlos, you seemed . . . well, like maybe I was being overcautious. What's your opinion? Maybe you've had more experience with this kind of project than I thought."

■ "Vic, you seemed a little upset when I suggested a deadline of June 12th. What else do you have going on?"

■ "What about your budgetary authority, Sam? Did I detect a fleeting look of 'This'll never work?!' across your face? What concerns do you have about it?"

■ "Ahn, you looked worried when I recommended the 'zero defects' goal. Am I right? If so, let's talk about it—what are your expectations?"

With your encouragement, your delegatee may be quite straightforward. However, don't assume all is well if a delegatee has voiced one concern and you've answered it. Always check again by saying something like:

■ "What other concerns (or questions) do you have?"

■ "Is there anything else you'd like to talk about?"

Once your delegatee decides to be honest with you, reinforce that candor by listening carefully without interrupting or getting defensive. Then it's your turn to be honest in the way you negotiate and resolve problems with your delegatee.

Determining Level of Authority

All of the items on the Delegation Issues worksheet are important, but #8 is perhaps the most important—understanding and agreeing on the level of authority the employee will have. If the delegatee leaves your meeting with a misunderstanding about this issue, you may have to pay a high price for it, as the following example illustrates:

■ Lana was excited about being asked to recommend PCs to be purchased for their department; she had definite ideas about the features she and her coworkers needed. But now she was being interrupted in the middle of the assignment by her boss.

"Lana, I just got a notice from OfficePro; it says that they shipped 17 Achieva computers to us today!"

"Great! Did they say when they'd arrive?"

"You mean this is true? Why didn't you talk it over with me?"

"I did! Remember last week, when I showed you how the Achieva outperformed all of its competitors? And you agreed that even though it was a little more expensive than other brands, it seemed to be the best choice for us?"

"Yes, but I didn't authorize you to order them! For one thing, why did you choose OfficePro?"

"Well, they'd just been really helpful."

"But you don't know if other companies sell the Achievas for less. And don't you remember my saying that the purchase would have to wait until next quarter, when we'd be in better financial shape?"

"All I know is that I thought I was authorized to get us the computers we need so badly, so I did. Sorry."

The price you or your delegatee pays for this misunderstanding may be in terms of dollars, a stinging embarrassment, resentment, or the failure of the project. So be sure the two of you are clear about how much authority the delegatee will have!

> If the delegatee leaves your meeting with a misunderstanding regarding his or her level of authority, you could pay a high price.

5

Getting It Down on Paper

Remember how you explored your thoughts and jotted them down on your Delegation Issues Worksheet? That was for *you*. Now, it's time to prepare a more condensed version of the worksheet that you can use to guide your discussion with your delegatee.

Before the meeting, fill in any information you plan to deliver to the delegatee—facts about what the purpose of the delegation is, why you've chosen this employee, what the goals are, and so on.

Then photocopy the worksheet, and as you discuss the assignment with your employee and come to agreement on various issues, you can both fill in the details. These include what training the employee will attend, what work will be reprioritized or reassigned, how much authority the employee will have, when the interim checkpoints will be, and so on.

You may wish to make copies of this form before you complete it so that you can use them for future delegations. Or you may wish to create your own form and then customize it for each new delegation.

Delegation Worksheet

Task: _____

Delegatee: _____

1. THE ASSIGNMENT
   a. Purpose of the task:

   _____

   b. How it relates to the goals of our area or organization:

   _____

   c. How the job has been done in the past (if it has):

   _____

   d. Why it's being delegated now:

   _____

   e. When it will begin:

   _____

   f. Your attitude about changes/improvements in how it's done:

   _____

2. BENEFITS
   a. Why delegatee was chosen, and why delegator is confident s/he can do it:

   _____

   b. What previous experience will serve delegatee well:

   _____

   c. What benefits delegatee can expect:

   _____

continued on the next page

5

Delegation Worksheet *(continued)*

3. DELEGATEE'S PRESENT WORKLOAD
   a. Work that needs reprioritizing:

   _____

   b. Work that needs reassigning to someone else:

   _____

4. ADDITIONAL TRAINING
   a. Training needed:

   _____

   b. What training is available when:

   _____

5. GOALS
   a. Results which must be achieved:

   _____

   b. How results will be measured and performance be evaluated:

   _____

6. CONSTRAINTS
   • Constraints (if any) on how the job should be done:

   _____

7. SURPRISES
   a. Any unusual circumstances or "danger points" which could crop up:

   _____

   b. How they might be avoided:

   _____

   c. What delegatee should do if they occur:

   _____

continued on the next page

Delegation Worksheet *(continued)*

8. DEGREE OF AUTHORITY
    a. What resources delegatee will control:

    _____

    b. New reporting relationships or lines of communication associated with this assignment:

    _____

    c. Other people delegatee will work with or interview:

    _____

    d. People to whom the delegator should talk or write to explain the delegation and request support:

    _____

    e. The types of decisions delegatee may make:

    _____

    Types which should be made by delegator or someone else:

    _____

    f. Under what circumstances the delegator will review the delegatee's work:

    _____

9. DEADLINES
    a. Final deadline:

    _____

    b. When we will review the completed project together:

    _____

10. CHECKPOINTS
    •   Points in the assignment when we will review progress on the delegation:

    _____

5

Chapter Summary

During the delegation meeting, the delegator and the delegatee develop a shared understanding about expectations for the assignment. One of the best ways a supervisor can establish understanding is to encourage feedback from the delegatee.

Feedback may be nonverbal, relying on facial expressions or body language, or it may be verbal, taking the form of a comment or question. If a delegatee's facial expression or body language appears confused or hesitant, encourage the delegatee to discuss his or her concerns. Some common areas of concern for delegatees include:

♦ Confusion regarding the task.

♦ Lack of experience.

♦ Disagreement with the assignment.

You can use open-ended questions to encourage the delegatee to express concerns and then work with the delegatee to resolve them.

Level of authority is the most critical issue a supervisor must resolve with a delegatee. Be sure the delegatee understands what he or she can do alone and what must be approved by you.

You and your delegatee may find it helpful to record the results of your meeting on paper. You can adapt the Delegation Issues Worksheet to use during your meeting with the delegatee, or you can develop your own form.

Self-Check: Chapter Five Review

Answers for these questions appear on page 116.

1. One of the best ways to be sure you and your delegatee understand each other is to ask for _____ from your delegatee.

2. True or False?
   If you pick up signs during the delegation meeting that a delegatee seems confused or hesitant, you should try to ignore them so you don't embarrass the delegatee.

3. Three common areas of concern that delegatees frequently express during the delegation meeting are:

   a. _____

   b. _____

   c. _____

4. What does asking a delegatee to paraphrase the explanation of an assignment do?

   _____

   _____

5. What is the most critical issue a supervisor must work out with a delegatee?

   _____

5

Chapter *Six*

Following Up with Delegatees

Chapter Objectives

▶ Complete a Work in Progress worksheet to track delegatees' progress.

▶ Explain the importance of supporting delegatees as originally agreed.

▶ Know what sort of help four types of delegatees are likely to need from you.

▶ Explain why it's important to allow employees to solve their own problems.

Whitney was excited to share some good news with Pat: "Delegation is great!" she exclaimed. "I gave assignments to three people a few weeks ago, and now, for the first time in years, I'm leaving the office on time!"

"Good for you!" Pat responded. "Delegating to three different people—you really jumped in with both feet. So how are they doing?"

"Doing?" Whitney asked in surprise. "Fine, I suppose. I would have heard if they were having trouble, right?"

"Maybe, maybe not," Pat replied. "Did you build in checkpoints? When did you and your delegatees decide you'd meet with them the first time?"

"In two weeks," Whitney said, opening her planner. "Gee, I've been so busy, I forgot to meet with them. Well, they must have forgotten, too—they haven't said anything!"

"And how about clearing the way?" Pat asked. "Did you make some calls to the people that your delegatees need to work with or get information from?"

> "You cannot mandate productivity, you must provide the tools to let people become their best."
>
> —*Steve Jobs*

"Oh, no! I forgot to do that, too!" Whitney said, shaking her head. "I'm starting to think that it was easier when I was doing everything—at least all I had to keep track of was myself!"

Have you ever made this mistake? It's a common one— concentrating on careful preparation and communication, then neglecting the follow-up steps that ensure success.

To return to our tandem bicycle metaphor, the delegatee has taken the front seat, and the delegator is sitting in back. But in Whitney's case, her delegatees are eagerly pumping away while she's distracted by the scenery. That means extra hard pedaling for her delegatees as they labor on their own to get to the destination. As you imagine, with no support from the delegator, delegatees soon get tired and discouraged.

> **With no support from the delegator, delegatees soon get tired and discouraged.**

Supervisors can avoid this pitfall by consistently tracking their delegatees' progress and providing ongoing support.

Tracking Progress

As a delegator, you have to keep an eye not only on what your delegatees have promised to do but also on what *you* have promised to do. If your delegations are few or simple, perhaps you can keep track of them with a few notes in your planner or an uncomplicated tickler file. Jot down the assignments you must complete ("Talk to Terry—Omar needs stats") and when you must complete them. Then jot down all the checkpoints you and your delegatee agreed to—those dates when you'll review progress on the project. Don't forget the final due date.

6

However, if you have several delegations in progress, these simple notations may not be adequate. The following Work in Progress worksheet will help you remember who (including yourself) is assigned to do what by when so you can be sure your delegations stay on track.

Once again, if you feel this worksheet would be useful, *photocopy it before filling it in.* Or let this form be a catalyst for your own great ideas, and create your own worksheet!

Work in Progress

Date	Delegation/Assignment	Delegatee # 1 2 3 4 5 6	Due Date	Done Date
____	_____	_ _ _ _ _ _	_____	_____
____	_____	_ _ _ _ _ _	_____	_____
____	_____	_ _ _ _ _ _	_____	_____
____	_____	_ _ _ _ _ _	_____	_____
____	_____	_ _ _ _ _ _	_____	_____
____	_____	_ _ _ _ _ _	_____	_____
____	_____	_ _ _ _ _ _	_____	_____
____	_____	_ _ _ _ _ _	_____	_____
____	_____	_ _ _ _ _ _	_____	_____
____	_____	_ _ _ _ _ _	_____	_____
____	_____	_ _ _ _ _ _	_____	_____
____	_____	_ _ _ _ _ _	_____	_____

Delegatee Key:

1: _____   2: _____   3: _____

4: _____   5: _____   6: _____

Here's how to use it:

After your delegation meeting, begin by writing today's date in the left-hand column. Then jot down the assignment. Do NOT record the details of the entire delegation—you've already recorded them on your Delegation Issues worksheet.

On the Work in Progress sheet, write what you're checking or reviewing on what date. Or what task the delegatee is to have completed and turned in to you on a certain date. That way, each day you can glance at the "Due Date" column and be reminded of what should be rolling in.

As you can see, you write your delegatees' names at the bottom of the sheet, keyed to a number. Then you just checkmark the appropriate squares on the sheet to indicate whose assignment is whose. Not only do these little boxes save room on the form, but they also reveal at a glance whether you're delegating to your employees with equal frequency or favoring one or two people. By the way, you may wish to designate yourself as #1 so that the promises you have made and the assignments you must complete will be quickly visible when you glance at the worksheet.

Because people don't always complete tasks by their due dates, the column on the far right has space for you to record what date that assignment or task was actually finished. Following is an example of a completed Work in Progress form

Work in Progress

Date	Delegation/Assignment	Delegation # 1	2	3	4	5	6	Due Date	Done Date
1/10	Ask Terry to help Omar with stats.	X						1/12	1/12
1/10	Ask Bev to give Tu any help he needs.	X						1/12	1/12
1/11	Report on outcome of City Council meeting.				X			1/15	1/15
1/12	Rewrite filing procedures.		X					1/19	
1/12	Get bids on whiteboards.						X	2/1	
1/13	Conduct emergency procedures drill.			X				1/25	
1/14	Turn in first draft of tuition refund policy.					X		2/1	
1/17	Turn in results of employee survey.						X	2/1	
1/17	Report results of team brainstorming session.				X			1/19	
1/19	Get bids on printing brochures.		X					2/4	
1/20	Meet on project's final results.			X				2/7	

Delegatee Key:
1: Myself   2: Omar   3: Gale   4: Frankie   5: Tu   6: Rebecca

6

Providing Support: How Much Is Enough?

■ When Chris gave John the opportunity to write a speech for the vice president, John jumped at the chance. In his former job, he'd often written similar speeches, and Chris told John that she knew he was good at it. They'd agreed that John would turn in a rough draft in two weeks after he'd researched the topic and created an outline. Yet here was Chris, only two days later, stopping by John's cubicle to ask how he was doing.

In reality, Chris was just passing through and thought she'd stop by to see if John needed anything from her. But when a delegator is more "supportive" than the delegatee expects, what message does it send to the delegatee?

■ Pavel's higher-ups have been leaning on him to reorganize the company into teams. He turned to his employee Jan, who expressed an interest in the idea at a staff meeting. Pavel assigned Jan to investigate how other organizations have made the transition to teams, and report her findings and a recommendation back to him.

Today's the deadline, but a few minutes before their scheduled meeting, Pavel had to dash out and handle a crisis elsewhere. Jan arrived, excited to share the results of her work, only to be greeted by an empty office.

Take a Moment

In the first example, what message did Chris's actions send to John?

_____

_____

In the second example, what message did Pavel's actions send to Jan?

_____

_____

Agreeing on the Level of Support

Delegators must be careful about the message they send their delegatees. A supervisor who provides too much support may inadvertently send the message that she or he doesn't trust the delegatee. A supervisor who provides too little support may send the message that she or he doesn't care about the assignment. How does a supervisor know how much support a delegatee needs? The best way to find out is to ask.

The delegation meeting is the place to discuss how much guidance you'll provide for the delegatee. How much support (based on his or her knowledge, past experience, and confidence) does your delegatee *want?* How much support do you believe she or he *needs?* Only when the two of you have resolved these questions to your mutual satisfaction do you record on your Delegation Worksheet what and when you need to review with the delegatee.

> **Once you've agreed on the checkpoints and the amount of support you'll provide, you need to stick by your agreement.**

Once you've agreed on the checkpoints and the amount of support you'll provide, you need to stick by your agreement and offer precisely that amount of support. Even if you *accidentally* offer more or less, that change in your implicit contract with the delegatee can cause problems, as the two previous examples illustrate.

So be careful of simply "stopping by to say 'hi'" to a delegatee who is confidently carrying out an assignment. And be sure you keep your appointments with a delegatee who's expecting to meet with you.

Of course, situations will arise that make you realize that you should be guiding and reviewing more (or less) often than you and the delegatee originally thought. For instance, in your desire to see your delegatee be successful, you may initially have provided a great deal of support. But now that both of you have more confidence, you can ask if there's any reason why the delegatee shouldn't take more action and make more decisions on his or her own. On the other hand, if you feel you need to pull in the reins, then express your concerns and explain why you'd like to review progress more often or make a decision with the delegatee.

6

Determining the Type of Support Needed

Besides the amount of support, you'll also need to determine the type of support your individual delegatees need. As you work with your delegatees, you'll discover that these needs will vary based on your delegatees' personality traits.

Remember, in Chapter Three we identified four different personality traits:

- Introvert

- Extrovert

- People-oriented

- Task-oriented

Identifying how these personality traits work together in your delegatees will help you predict what sort of follow-up you'll need to do as they work on the assignment you've delegated to them.

Supporting Introverted People-Oriented Employees

Introverted people-oriented employees are especially supportive of their coworkers.

Believe it or not, it is possible to be both introverted and people-oriented. These employees are quiet and good with details, yet value human relationships and are especially supportive of their coworkers. They are loyal, caring, and want to contribute to their team. Because they are people oriented, they'll probably look forward to your "checkpoint" meetings as a way of staying connected, sharing ideas, and making sure they're on the right track.

What Introverted People-Oriented Employees Want from You

- Clearly defined goals, roles, and expectations (all your delegatees deserve these!)

- Assistance in analyzing problems and making decisions (especially those impacting people)

- Assistance in meeting deadlines

- Assistance in taking necessary risks

Be prepared to explain goals and roles clearly and carefully; that will provide the reassurance these employees need. At problem-solving time, ask these employees where they're "stuck," and help them analyze the strengths and weaknesses of various courses of action in a step-by-step manner.

Although introverted people-oriented employees are conscientious, their love of people can prevent them from meeting deadlines—they may promise too much to too many! Warn them at the outset to avoid doing so, and urge them to be honest with you about whether they can make the deadlines you two discuss. Then as you follow up, be on the lookout for signs that they've become buried in commitments they can't keep; you may need to step in and help them dig their way out.

Finally, reassure these employees that taking risks is sometimes necessary—and sometimes it even opens up opportunities!

By the way, of the four types, the introverted people-oriented type is the one most likely to welcome and respond to your coaching, so your efforts can really make a difference! As these employees develop, you'll be able to be less involved; just "catch" them doing things right and express your confidence in them.

Supporting Extroverted People-Oriented Employees

These employees are likable, energetic workers. They will thrive if you give them people-related assignments that allow them to verbalize their ideas, help others, and motivate people. As they work, their social skills, ability to see the big picture, and creativity will serve them well.

What Extroverted People-Oriented Employees Want from You
These employees won't ask for your advice much, but they would like you to give them the following:

◆ Freedom from detail, which you may or may not be able to grant

◆ Freedom from control, which you should be able to give them once you're confident they can work without it

◆ Appreciation for their efforts, which you should be able to muster!

> Extroverted people-oriented employees like people-related assignments that allow them to verbalize their skills.

6

If these employees do need to deal with detail on an assignment, remind them of its importance and encourage them to do one thing at a time carefully to ensure accuracy.

Extroverted people-oriented employees may also benefit from some time-management advice from you. They often under-estimate how long it will take to accomplish a task, and because they usually let people interrupt them, they're likely to miss some deadlines or come in exactly on time, having worked all night to finish the project.

Remind these employees to build in more time than they think they'll need, to break down the project into many small steps, and then to assign interim checkpoints to those small steps. Then monitor their progress to make sure they're moving along!

Extroverted people-oriented employees will see you more as a friend/mentor than an authority figure, and you may find that you feel the need to have checkpoint meetings more than they do. Once you're confident that they've overcome their weaknesses, they'll occupy very little of your time.

Supporting Introverted Task-Oriented Employees

These employees bring thoroughness and high-quality accuracy to any project. Their unemotional, data-driven approach will serve your organization well in projects that require precision and planning.

> **Introverted task-oriented employees bring thoroughness and high-quality accuracy to any project.**

What Introverted Task-Oriented Employees Want from You

◆ A clearly defined task and detailed operating standards

◆ A quiet, organized environment

◆ Plenty of time to complete the assignment to their standards, which you may not be able to provide

◆ Limited risk, which you also may not be able to promise

Introverted task-oriented employees often have difficulty with deadlines because of their insistence on perfection. Again, have frequent checkpoint meetings to be sure they're making progress. When possible, remind them that they don't need to investigate 20 courses of action or proofread a document 20 times!

Because introverted task-oriented employees are not "people persons," you may have to remind them that process can be as important as product—and that they need to be more sensitive to others' feelings or listen to their perspective.

Like introverted people-oriented employees, these employees may initially take much more of your time than you'd anticipated asking questions and voicing fears. Keep reassuring them, and eventually, they'll be on their way.

Supporting Extroverted Task-Oriented Employees

These employees are eager to get the job done! Motivated by a good challenge, they are organized, decisive, and very direct.

What Extroverted Task-Oriented Employees Want from You
These employees have strong ideas about what they'd like from you:

◆ Direct, logical answers to questions

◆ Autonomy and authority

◆ Challenging and varied assignments

◆ Opportunity for advancement

If you can give them these things, great! Certainly you can answer questions directly rather than spending time in idle chitchat. However, you may need to help them learn that some controls are needed, and they can accomplish a lot even if they're not the final authority. (Everyone has a boss, even you!)

You may also need to help these employees realize that though not all assignments can be challenging or even varied, it's still important to do them well. When you can't promise advancement, you can promise valuable visibility and recognition for a job well done.

> **Extroverted task-oriented employees are organized, decisive, and very direct.**

6

While they may not realize it, extroverted task-oriented employees also need to learn that sometimes they'll accomplish results *faster* by going *slower*. Advise them to solicit ideas from others, hear them out, and explain why they've reached a conclusion rather than just ordering them around or charging out of the room.

Because this personality type is assertive (sometimes aggressive) and task-focused, they will want to meet with you less often than the other three and be the most difficult to direct. For these employees, a meaningful compliment is not your praise— it's your giving them more freedom. Nevertheless, insist on periodic meetings until you feel they're capable of taking the reins.

Take a Moment

Think of an employee to whom you have delegated work in the past. Which of the descriptions just given does that person seem to fit? Based on what you've just read, how will you now provide support and guidance for this person?

_____

_____

_____

_____

_____

_____

Developing Your Delegatees' Abilities and Initiative

As you've seen, different delegatees approach problems differently. However, supervisors should help every delegatee develop a positive attitude and a set of skills to cope with problems.

Here are five ways an employee could face a problem. They lead from a no-ownership level to a high-ownership level.

The Problem Ownership Ladder

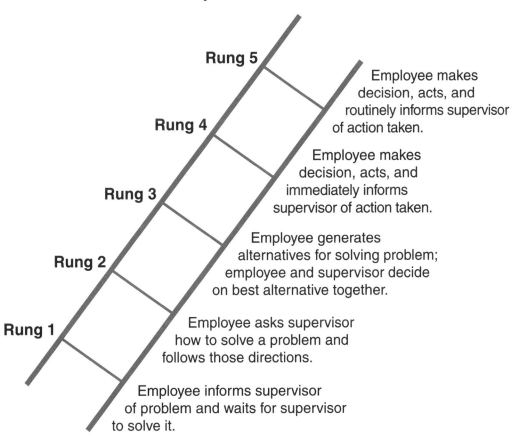

Rung 5 — Employee makes decision, acts, and routinely informs supervisor of action taken.

Rung 4 — Employee makes decision, acts, and immediately informs supervisor of action taken.

Rung 3 — Employee generates alternatives for solving problem; employee and supervisor decide on best alternative together.

Rung 2 — Employee asks supervisor how to solve a problem and follows those directions.

Rung 1 — Employee informs supervisor of problem and waits for supervisor to solve it.

6

In hectic times, you will be tempted to take over and quickly solve the problem *for* the delegatee. But making a decision yourself and explaining it to delegatees won't help them grow. It's only when delegatees get the experience of solving problems that they develop their abilities and initiative. And as they become proficient at solving problems and move up the ownership ladder, you're freed up to solve the larger problems that you rarely had time to tackle before.

Make it clear to your delegatees that the two lowest rungs of the ownership ladder are not options for them!

Therefore, make it clear to your delegatees that the two lowest rungs of the ownership ladder are *not* options for them! Instruct them that when they encounter a dilemma or a difficulty, they should climb to the third rung (your more introverted delegatees will need more encouragement than the extroverted ones).

Insist that no problem be brought to your attention unless it's accompanied by at least a couple of alternatives to solve it. Then you can discuss those alternatives, along with the advantages and disadvantages of each as you perceive them, and together, you and the delegatee can come to a decision.

Once you've coached and authorized your employees to act at level four or five in various situations, you'll realize that the time you spent training and developing them was a wise investment for you, them, and your company.

Chapter Summary

After delegating an assignment to an employee, it's important to follow up to be sure the job gets done effectively and efficiently. Tracking assignments on a Work in Progress form will remind you of what you and your delegatees have agreed to and whether you're both meeting your deadlines and goals.

Monitor your delegatees' progress by checking on them no more or less than the two of you originally discussed so you don't interfere or ignore developing problems. (You can always renegotiate the degree and frequency of support, if need be.)

The type of support you give your delegatees will vary according to their personalities and your own. In any case, encourage them to develop a feeling of "ownership" in their assignments versus simply "leasing with option to buy."

When problems arise, require delegatees to bring you not just the problem, but suggestions for solving it as well. Remember, your own supervisor or manager will evaluate you on how well you develop others, not how well you solve every problem yourself.

6

Self-Check: Chapter Six Review

Answers to the following questions appear on pages 117–118.

1. As a delegator, you have to keep an eye not only on what your _____ have promised to do but also on what _____ have promised to do.

2. What type of message may a supervisor who provides too much support inadvertently send?

   _____

3. What type of message may a supervisor who provides too little support inadvertently send?

   _____

4. What will delegatees with these personality traits want or need from you? Match the action you need to take with the personality type.

   _____ Introverted People-Oriented

   _____ Extroverted People-Oriented

   _____ Introverted Task-Oriented

   _____ Extroverted Task-Oriented

   a. A reminder that process is as important as product
   b. Freedom from detail
   c. Autonomy and authority
   d. Clearly defined goals, roles, and expectations

5. The Problem Ownership Ladder has five rungs, or levels, that represent five ways of facing a problem. Which levels should not be options for your delegatees?

   _____

   _____

6. Instead, what levels of the ladder should delegatees follow when they encounter a problem?

   _____

   _____

   _____

6

Chapter *Seven*

Coping with Delegation Difficulties

Chapter Objectives

▶ Respond effectively to the following situations:

- A delegatee who is headed for certain trouble

- An insecure delegatee who wants to give up on the assignment

- A lazy delegatee who tries to delegate the assignment back to you

- A flattering delegatee who is more concerned with pleasing you than with getting his or her own results

- An intimidating delegatee who insists s/he's too busy to take on a new assignment

- An egotistical employee who antagonizes others with his/her superior attitude

---

> "Freedom to make good decisions means freedom to make bad decisions."
> —*Management Theorist Rufus E. Miles, Jr.*

If you've applied the previous chapters' delegation techniques, congratulations! You and your delegatee are well on your way to a successful "tandem bicycle" experience. However, just as an unseen rut in the road has jolted and thrown many a bike and its riders, an unexpected difficulty can derail your delegation!

This chapter will prepare you for six such situations. After you read each scenario (and *before* you read the suggested response) decide what you would do in that situation. Then compare your response with the one suggested.

Learning from Mistakes

Let's say you're pedaling watchfully from the back seat of our metaphorical tandem bike. Suddenly you realize the delegatee is about to make a wrong turn. Do you apply your set of brakes? Urge him to swerve the other way? Or cover your eyes and pray?

In other words, in real life, when you see your delegatee headed for disaster, should you:

◆ Take over the delegation?

◆ Stop the delegatee and advise a change?

◆ Point out a potential problem and suggest that the delegatee consider a contingency plan?

◆ Discuss your concerns with the delegatee but leave any decisions about making changes to him or her?

◆ Do nothing and hope for the best?

If your answer is "It depends," you're right. Different situations dictate different responses.

Generally, you should allow your delegatee to make a mistake if you believe the cost won't be too high to bear. Your decision may depend on two things:

◆ **How much will the delegatee learn from making the mistake?**
Often, making a mistake will drill home a lesson in a far stronger way than a lecture ever could. However, the delegatee may not learn from the error. He or she may be too defensive to accept responsibility for the action or too humiliated to recover from it. As a supervisor, can you predict how your employee will handle the situation?

◆ **How costly will the mistake be to your organization?**
If it's just a matter of a few dollars that you can afford to spend, let the delegatee make the mistake. On the other hand, if it's a large amount of money, or a matter of legal liability or your organization's reputation, you'll want to step in.

If you decide to intervene, explain your concern to the delegatee and ask if he or she agrees. If the delegatee does agree, ask if he or she can think of another course of action to avert the situation. If the delegatee truly can't think of any alternatives, you can suggest a course of action.

> Generally, you should allow your delegatee to make a mistake if you believe the cost won't be too high to bear.

7

What if you express a concern and the delegatee doesn't agree that it could be a problem? Then you've either got to be a very persuasive communicator, articulating the risks clearly and vividly, or you've got to take a chance on the delegatee's own course of action. Only in true emergencies should you take the assignment away from the delegatee.

Take a Moment

Can you think of an occasion when you took an assignment back from someone who was headed for trouble? Describe it below.

_____

_____

How might you handle a similar situation in the future?

_____

_____

Building Confidence

You've delegated a job to Sarah because she's a hard worker. It's a challenging assignment, but you're sure she can handle it. Yet here she is a few days later, wanting to climb off your metaphorical tandem bike for good!

■ "I just don't think I'm cut out for this—the whole thing seems overwhelming to me!" she explains. "Maybe in another year I'll be ready for an assignment like this one, but for now, could you just give it to someone else?"

Sarah lacks confidence, pure and simple. What might you do in this situation?

Think back to the delegation meeting: Did you discuss all the items on the Delegation Worksheet so Sarah understands why you chose her and how much authority she has? Did you give her all the information that will help her succeed? And even if you thought you explained the details well, are you sure she absorbed them and understood them? If there's any doubt, go over those issues again so she feels better prepared to do the job.

Also, if you can tolerate Sarah's doing a less-than-perfect job, assure her that you have confidence in her abilities, that you want her to do her best with the assignment, and that you'll support whatever results she delivers.

On the other hand, if you feel that this assignment just may be too daunting for her, consider breaking it into smaller, easier jobs that she can share with you or another employee. Then coach her carefully along the way. That way, she'll build her self-confidence with each success.

> **Assure delegatees who lack confidence that you believe they can do the job.**

Take a Moment

Can you think of an occasion when you took an assignment back from someone who didn't feel confident enough to do it? Describe it below.

_____

_____

How might you handle a similar situation in the future?

_____

_____

7

Developing Responsibility

Picture your delegatees confronting you with the following situations:

■ "Say, boss, we've got a problem! I was working on the catalog late last night—just finishing it up—when the hard drive crashed. I was going to make a backup before I left the office, but the crash came just before that. So what should we do? Do you want to think about it this morning, and then give me a call when you've decided how to fix it?"

■ "Well, I was going to attend that meeting in your place last night, but when I got there, no one was there! Guess they moved it to a different location, but who knew? Well, sorry. Maybe you can call Yoshi from ComRax to find out what happened. She was going to attend, and I hear she takes good notes."

What do these two situations have in common, and how should you respond?

In both of these situations, your delegatee is trying the old "reverse delegation" play! Suddenly, through a subtle or not-so-subtle transaction, the delegator is expected to fix the problem. Sometimes the transfer of responsibility occurs so smoothly that the two hardly realize it's happened. In tandem bicycle language, the delegator finds him- or herself in firm possession of a bike with a flat tire, while the delegatee shrugs and saunters away!

Why do employees pull this annoying reverse delegation? It's possible that they're just avoiding *all* extra work. Or maybe they never wanted this assignment in the first place, and they're hoping you'll get frustrated with them and take it back. (Did you point out the benefits of successfully completing the assignment?)

Don't let delegatees "reverse delegate" their work back to you.

You offered support and guidance to your employee when you gave the assignment, but taking the job back from someone who just doesn't want to do it benefits neither of you. In an article for *Harvard Business Review,* William Oncken and Donald Wass, executives of the William Oncken Corporation, recommend that supervisors advise employees: "At no time while I am helping you with this or any other problem will your problem become my problem. The instant your problem becomes mine, you will no longer have a problem. I cannot help a person who hasn't got a problem."

So don't let your delegatees walk away from a bike with a flat tire. Your work-averse employees can become competent, confident decision makers if you insist that they actually do the job! In other words, there's nothing like changing one's own flat tire to develop confidence and a sense of ownership!

> ## Take a Moment
>
> Can you think of an occasion when you allowed a "reverse delegation" because you could do the job faster or better? Describe it below.
>
> _____
>
> _____
>
> How might you handle a similar situation in the future?
>
> _____
>
> _____

Solving Problems Independently

Let's say you're pedaling along, content to let the front biker (your delegatee) make decisions about the route. Yet every few feet, he's asking for your approval or floating trial balloons, since "You're the expert!"

In real life, it looks like this:

Sam welcomed his assignment, but ever since, he hasn't made a move without first asking what you'd do in this situation. It's flattering that he asks your opinion and cares about doing the job right, but you're getting tired of his second-guessing. You suspect that gaining experience and achieving results are taking a back seat to his simply pleasing and complimenting you!

How can you get Sam to take risks, make his own decisions, and thus profit from the delegation experience?

Begin by asking yourself a tough question: Might you have unwittingly trained Sam (and other employees) to be helpless? That is, do you rarely give employees a chance to solve problems or make decisions? Have you unintentionally communicated the message that when employees don't solve a problem as *you* would have, they've failed? That sort of supervision can produce employees who are insecure, apathetic, or even hostile. No wonder they end up deferring to you!

7

Encourage employees to solve problems on their own.

To retrain people like Sam, do two things:

◆ Always talk about the *result* you want rather than the *methods.*

◆ Think "Ask—Don't Tell!" When delegatees ask, "Where do we go from here?" answer, "Where do *you* think *you* should go from here?" When they ask, "What would you like done at this point?" ask, "What do *you* think is the best course of action?" (See more details in Chapter 6.) This technique is as old as Socrates, whose goal was to make students think for themselves. And critical thinking, by its very nature, develops initiative!

Remember, your goal is to strengthen decision-making skills in your employees and to free up some time for yourself in the process. When delegatees run to you for your approval every step of the way, both goals are compromised.

Take a Moment

Can you think of an occasion when a delegatee flattered you into making decisions that he or she should have made? Describe it below.

_____

_____

How might you handle a similar situation in the future?

_____

_____

Reducing Complaints

Squeaky wheels generally get grease, right? This metaphor suggests that if people complain loudly and irritatingly enough, someone will fix things for them. In real life, our squeaky wheel looks like this:

■ Carla acted a bit hostile when you gave her the assignment, even though you complimented her about how capable she was. She suggested that you should really be doing this yourself—that she was already far too busy to take on anything else. You continued, explaining the issues on your Delegation Worksheet, and when you finished, she nodded curtly and left. Now when you see her in the halls, she won't even make eye contact. You suspect she hasn't started the assignment.

How can you handle people like Carla?

We all develop our people skills through a lifetime of experimentation. For chronic squeaky wheels, trial and error have taught them one thing—complaining works! You may not be able to change how Carla interacts with others, but you can teach her that her tactics no longer work with you. Begin by sitting down with Carla again. Reexplain why this job is important to you and the organization and how her own career will benefit if she does the assignment well.

Don't give in to chronic complainers.

If she's still sulking, remind her cheerfully that it's up to you to decide who does what jobs, and you've decided this one's for her. In other words, don't allow her to intimidate you—don't respond to her glowering by groveling!

7

As a last resort, point out the consequences of not accepting the assignment or intentionally doing it badly.

No matter how you get Carla back on the job, begin to build a more positive relationship by "catching" her doing things right and praising her. She may learn that taking responsibility and earning compliments is a lot more fun than avoiding responsibility and earning criticism. In time, the once-squeaky wheel may become one of your best employees!

Take a Moment

Can you think of an occasion when a delegatee intimidated or manipulated you into taking back an assignment? Describe it below.

_____

_____

How might you handle a similar situation in the future?

_____

_____

Working with the Team

Counsel delegatees to maintain good relationships with team members.

You're pedaling along from your backseat position while your capable delegatee zips confidently down the street. As he rolls proudly past pedestrians with his nose high in the air, you worry that he won't see the trip wire stretched out in front of the bike by those who don't appreciate his superior attitude.

In real life, your delegatee, Larry, sails along with an "I'm-the-chosen-one!" air. The good news is that he is quite capable; the bad news is that he's antagonizing everyone around him. Sooner or later, you're afraid that they'll sabotage his efforts in subtle ways.

What might you say to Larry?

Take Larry aside, and describe how others perceive him. Don't make broad statements like "You have a bad attitude," or "You act like you don't need the rest of the team"—that will only put him on the defensive. Instead, describe specific behaviors you have observed and people's reaction to them:

■ "Yesterday, you told Maria her idea was no good without even giving her a chance to explain it. When you do things like that, the other team members think that you don't care about anyone's opinion except your own."

If Larry insists that he hasn't *told* anyone that he feels he's better or smarter than they are, point out how loudly his nonverbal communication speaks *for* him. Explain to Larry that getting along with people is as much a part of his job as completing tasks. Point out how moving up in life often depends on interpersonal skills. Then provide frequent feedback or training. Once Larry begins to appreciate his coworkers' abilities, he'll see that they're willing to work with him rather than against him when he's in the driver's seat.

Take a Moment

Can you think of an occasion when a delegatee antagonized his or her coworkers by acting superior to them? Describe how you handled it below.

_____

_____

How might you handle a similar situation in the future?

_____

_____

Chapter Summary

Even when you've matched your delegation to the perfect employee, and you and the delegatee have had a productive discussion about the assignment, pitfalls can still pop up. Often, you can put the job back on the road to success by reviewing and clarifying the issues on your Delegation Worksheet. Sometimes, however, the problem isn't caused by a lack of clear communication; it's caused by an employee who feels unable or unwilling to complete (or even accept!) the assignment. At those times, applying specific strategies will usually help delegatees "climb aboard" once again.

7

Self-Check: Chapter Seven Review

Fill in the blanks with the appropriate word or phrase. Answers appear on page 118.

1. Your decision about whether to intervene when you see your delegatee headed for disaster should be based on two things:
   • How much the delegatee will _____ from making the mistake.
   • How _____ the mistake will be.

2. One way to help an employee build confidence is by _____ an assignment into smaller, easier _____ that can be _____ with you or another employee.

3. Your work-averse employees can become competent, confident decision-makers if you _____ that they actually _____ the job!

4. To get people to take risks, make their own decisions, and thus profit from the delegation experience, do two things:
   • Always talk about the _____ you want, rather than the _____.
   • Think "_____ — don't _____."

5. To get a "squeaky wheel" to stop complaining and accept an assignment, reexplain why the task is _____ and how it can _____ the delegatee's career. As a last resort, point out the _____ for not accepting the assignment or for intentionally doing it _____.

6. To get a superior-acting delegatee to work better with coworkers, describe how others _____ him or her, and explain that _____ _____ with people is as much a part of his or her job as completing tasks.

Notes

7

Chapter *Eight*

Evaluating the Completed Delegation: Celebrating Success, Learning from Failure

Chapter Objectives

▶ Explain the importance of sharing the credit or blame for the delegation's final results.

▶ Name two ways to recognize a delegatee's interim efforts and five ways to recognize final results.

▶ Name two ways to respond when a delegation fails and know when to use each.

▶ Explain the role of performance appraisals in the delegation process.

The data are assembled . . . the presentation is made . . . the project is completed. At some point, every type of delegation gets "signed, sealed, and delivered." And as word of the project and its results spread, scenes like these are played out:

> "There are no foolish questions and no man becomes a fool until he has stopped asking questions."
> — *Charles Steinmetz*

■ The executive vice president strode with purpose toward the manager. "Chris!" she began. "I just read that report you sent over, and I had to let you know in person—it's an impressive piece of work! Your in-depth analysis will allow us to make some well-informed decisions as we head into next year. So who gets the kudos? I heard your assistant played a key role in the research. What's his name?"

"Uh, well, I asked Tu for a few stats," Chris responded hesitantly, "but it was pretty much my work. I knew you'd want someone with my experience and judgment on the project. I'm just pleased to be able to make a contribution."

■ "Oh, there you are!" shouted the supermarket general manager to the produce manager. "What's the story with the produce? I knew you were going to rearrange some bins to improve the traffic flow, but instead you've taken us back to the Stone Age! Customers can't find what they're looking for, they're bumping into each other, the lettuce is all wilted . . . it's a disaster! How could you do this?"

"Well, I . . . uh . . . I *didn't* do it," the produce manager mumbled. "Lee did it. He, um, he just made the changes without talking them over with me, I guess."

"But you're his supervisor—did you give him the authority to move everything around without checking with you first?"

"Uh . . . no . . . I was out sick. That's it—I was home with the flu. Lee's really to blame here. I guess I can't trust him—he just can't handle responsibility."

Sharing the Credit—and the Blame

Some have said, "Delegation is a risk combined with an act of faith and trust." Delegators and delegatees need to share the credit or the blame for the delegation's final results in order to maintain that faith and trust. However, when it comes to sharing the kudos and facing up to the criticism, the delegators in the previous examples didn't prove very trustworthy!

In the first example, the delegator failed to give credit where credit was due! Returning to our tandem bicycle metaphor, this is like standing proudly at the finish line, directly *in front of* your partner as the *Newsweek* photographer snaps a picture! Aren't *both* of you are responsible for this resounding success?

In the second vignette, the delegator failed to accept the ultimate responsibility for the outcome of the job. That's like hopping off the bike while your partner in front is still pedaling, advising, "That's okay, just head for that cliff—I'll be along in a minute!"

When we're under pressure, we sometimes respond without thinking; later, we realize our mistake and regret what we've said or done.

> **Delegators and delegatees need to share the credit or the blame for a delegation's final results in order to maintain faith and trust.**

8

101

Take a Moment

If you took credit for your delegatee's impressive results, how might he or she feel? Why might you be sorry later?

_____

_____

What would be a better response to the vice president in the first example?

_____

_____

Giving Credit Where Credit Is Due

> **If you take credit for your delegatee's success, your delegatee will resent you for stealing the glory.**

If you take credit for your delegatee's success, your delegatee will resent your stealing something that belonged to him or her—the glory! And the lack of acknowledgement will be especially difficult for your delegatee to accept if you originally promised him or her public recognition, increased power and influence, or even career advancement.

Perhaps most importantly, your delegatee will be reluctant to take on future assignments when the extra effort from this one yielded so few benefits (and when the delegatee feels she or he works for a thief). Also, as your other employees hear what happened, they too may be unwilling to take on extra work.

When a delegatee succeeds, both of you have earned a spot in the limelight! Here's what the manager in our first example might have said to share it:

■ "My assistant's name is Tu Troung, and you heard right—he did play a key role in preparing the report. I've had my eye on him for several months, and I decided to give him a shot at this project. It took a little coaching, but I'm proud of his final product. I'm glad you're pleased with it, too."

Take a Moment

If you blamed a delegatee for mistakes (instead of monitoring the project closely to *prevent* mistakes or taking the responsibility for the final outcome), how might the person feel? Why might you be sorry later?

_____

_____

What would be a better response to the store manager in the example on page 101?

_____

_____

Accepting Your Share of the Blame

If you blame a delegatee for mistakes, how might the person feel? In a word, *betrayed.*

If you promised coaching to help your delegatee succeed with this assignment and then you abdicated your responsibility and allowed him or her to wander around blindly, you're guilty of not "walking your talk." This is hardly the kind of leadership you want to be known for.

> **If you blame a delegatee for mistakes, that person will feel betrayed.**

If you gave the delegatee full authority to take action and promised to support his decision, and then you blamed him or her for taking the *wrong* action, you're guilty of nothing less than treachery. You've made a mockery of the whole delegation process.

Your *former* delegatee will definitely avoid accepting assignments from you in the future and advise his or her coworkers to do the same. Some subtle (or not so subtle) sabotage may also begin to sneak into your area.

What would be a better response to the store manager in the second example? The answer depends on how much guidance and authority the produce manager actually did give Lee. Here's one possible response:

8

■ "I'm sorry—we'll get it corrected. I asked Lee to show me some ideas *on paper,* and he was working on those. But when I was out sick for a week, he got worried that we'd miss the deadline you'd set for changes in the produce department. So he just took a stab at one of his designs and rearranged the produce.

"Lee is a hard worker and *wants* to do well—I've got to give him points for initiative and creativity! But I didn't give him enough guidance. In retrospect, I think he should have just waited for me to return before making the changes, so we'll talk about that. For now, we'll change things back, and then we'll work together on some new alternatives."

Celebrating Success

When a delegatee successfully completes a delegation, celebrate!

Sharing credit is only one of the ways of rewarding a successful delegation effort. When an employee successfully completes a delegation, you can show your appreciation and boost employee morale by celebrating that success. And when you delegate a large project, celebrating the interim checkpoints along the way can help keep your delegatee motivated.

One of the most meaningful ways to recognize interim successes is your sincere "Thank you" and some specific remarks that indicate you know how hard your delegatee is working on the assignment. A kind word is nice; a written note is even better. Other effective ways include:

♦ Getting the delegatee's car washed over the lunch hour and tucking a "Thanks for your hard work" note under the windshield wiper.

♦ Taking the delegatee to lunch. Variations on this theme include giving a gift certificate for two to four for lunch or bringing the delegatee deluxe bagged lunches for a week.

♦ Sending an arrangement of fruit, flowers, balloons, or chocolates.

♦ Giving a gift certificate for a massage or sending a masseuse to the delegatee's office for a quick back, shoulder, and neck massage.

◆ Giving an afternoon (or more) off. Better yet, giving the delegatee a round of golf or tickets to a ballgame and a day off to enjoy it.

At the end of the project, you may wish to recognize the delegatee's achievement with something larger:

◆ Get T-shirts printed for those who worked on the project. ("I survived _____" or "The Extra Mile Club" or "MVPs of the ABC Project!")

◆ Send a letter of commendation to the delegatee and his or her personnel file.

◆ Throw a celebratory lunch or dinner in the delegatee's honor; then award a plaque or certificate to him or her.

◆ Be sure that the delegatee receives recognition (a note, phone call, or plaque) from your boss—or your boss's boss.

◆ Send a thank-you note to the delegatee's home to thank his or her family for their patience and support during this project.

◆ Give the delegatee a certificate for dinner and a night on the town for two—to top things off, add a limousine ride.

◆ Get the accomplishment written up in the company newsletter.

◆ Rent a sports car for the delegatee to drive for a week.

◆ Pay the delegatee's parking fees for a month (or a year!).

Since you want your gesture to be well received by the delegatee, choose the reward carefully. Consider your delegatee's personality: Is she or he rather shy? Then a big flashy public display is the wrong choice—a letter to his or her personnel file or family would be more appropriate. Is the delegatee outgoing? Then the celebratory dinner or the sports car may be just the ticket.

8

Perhaps your delegatee would welcome the paid parking fees or the time off to attend to personal matters. Unless you want to surprise the person, there's a surefire way to find out what reward would be most appreciated—ask.

Take a Moment

Think about one of the assignments you have given or will soon delegate. Now think about the delegatee. What are two ways you might recognize a job well done?

_____

_____

If it's a large project with interim checkpoints, what are two small ways to recognize his/her effort along the way?

_____

_____

Following Up from Failure

Unfortunately, not every delegation results in resounding success. How should you respond when the outcome is disappointing or downright botched? You have two choices:

A. If you believe the employee made a sincere effort to meet expectations, turn the experience into the best lesson you can. Analyze why and how problems cropped up, where the delegatee made mistakes, and how those mistakes can be avoided on the next assignment. Condemn the error but not the person who made it; focus on learning, not blame. In most cases, this is the preferable response. It's the obvious choice if you realize that the employee didn't have the skills you thought she or he did, if you weren't able to coach as carefully as you would have liked, or if unforeseen circumstances doomed the project.

B. If you believe the employee was negligent, use your company's disciplinary steps by applying anything from a reprimand to termination. Be careful with this option; use it only when you believe the delegatee has broken company policy or

> Try to turn failed delegations into learning experiences.

failed to make a good-faith effort to successfully complete the project. If you choose this option, make sure you're consistent and follow your organization's policies exactly.

Take a Moment

Consider the following four situations. Would they call for Response A (analyze how to avoid mistakes in the future) or Response B (take disciplinary action)? Write the letter in the blank, and check your answers on page 119.

1. Pat hated the fact that Gloria had done so badly at this assignment—she'd seemed so perfect for it when they first discussed it. However, several unforeseen circumstances had cropped up, and now that he thought about it, he realized it was surprising that she'd done as well as she had.
   A or B? _____

2. Gail was disappointed in Carlos. She'd made it clear that he had spending authority of $500, and yet he'd ordered $6,000 worth of computer equipment without informing her. Now here it was, delivered and installed.
   A or B? _____

3. Juan had been excited about the project he'd assigned to Ben, but apparently his enthusiasm had not been contagious! Week after week, Ben missed deadlines. When Juan asked him what was going on, he just shrugged and said he had "other stuff" he had to do first. Yet he never seemed to make an honest effort to start the project, much less complete it.
   A or B? _____

4. Whitney thought Sonya had potential, so she chose her for an assignment that would stretch her current skills. Although she didn't protest the assignment, Sonya was quite anxious about it. Her fear of convening focus groups, interviewing people, and then presenting the results of her study to the higher-ups prevented her from doing the kind of professional job that Whitney had hoped for.
   A or B? _____

8

Learning from the Delegation

When the delegated assignment is complete, you may be tempted to climb off the tandem bike and never ride it again— at least not with this particular partner! But because experience is such a valuable teacher, you shouldn't simply walk away empty-handed. Whether the results of the delegation were positive or negative, both you and the delegatee will profit from a debriefing meeting in which you make a careful play-by-play analysis of what occurred.

> **Whether the results of the delegation were positive or negative, both you and the delegatee will profit from a debriefing meeting.**

Together with the delegatee, review the Delegation Worksheet the two of you followed at your initial meeting. Using it to remind you of the issues that guided your discussion, ask yourselves some questions:

◆ Where were we right on track?

◆ Where would we make some adjustments?

◆ What bottlenecks could we eliminate next time?

You may want to concentrate on the following issues from the worksheet:

Goals

◆ Were the goals and performance measurements reasonable?

Constraints

◆ Were those constraints really necessary?

◆ Should there have been additional constraints?

Surprises

◆ Were we blindsided by any *additional* surprises?

◆ Is there some way we could avoid being blindsided in the future?

Degree of Authority

◆ Did the delegatee have enough authority?

◆ What decisions might she or he now be able to make that previously needed approval from the delegator or someone else?

◆ Were there occasions when the delegatee had too much authority?

Deadlines

◆ Were the deadlines appropriate to the project?

◆ If not, how might we set better ones in the future?

Checkpoints

◆ Were the checkpoints (both the number and the dates of checkpoints) appropriate to the project?

◆ If not, how might we set better ones in the future?

You should also ask your delegatee for specific feedback on your performance as a delegator. Encourage your delegatee to speak freely by asking open-ended questions such as:

◆ "What did you like about how we worked together on this project?"

◆ "What wasn't so good?"

◆ "What would you change about how we work together the next time you take on a project?"

Before your debriefing meeting ends, there's one more important question to ask your delegatee:

◆ "What additional responsibilities are you interested in that would help you grow and become more valuable to the company?"

Use the delegatee's answer to help you plan future delegation assignments.

8

Seeking Additional Feedback

After you've had a chance to think about what you learned at the debriefing meeting, you can learn even more about delegation by talking to two important people—your supervisor and yourself!

If the person you report to is a good delegator, give an account of your delegation to him or her. Don't be shy about telling your supervisor where and how the experience was successful and what you learned from it. Then ask for pointers—what might you do even better in the future?

As your final step in the feedback process, seek out the wisdom of that all-important judge—yourself. Finish processing the delegation by reflecting on the following:

◆ What did this delegation do for me?

◆ What did I learn about delegation?

◆ What did I learn about myself?

◆ How much time (if any) did I save?

◆ What did I do with that time?

◆ How can I further improve my delegation skills?

Using the Performance Appraisal to Evaluate Delegation

What do performance appraisals have to do with the process of evaluating a completed delegation? They give you an opportunity to step back and consider not just one delegation, but the cumulative effect of several delegations with your employees.

When you evaluate any one delegation with the delegatee, it's easy to skip over the larger issues. A formal appraisal gives you a chance to discuss:

◆ How the employee is developing.

◆ How he or she is contributing to the company's goals.

◆ What the future looks like.

It's also an excellent time to ask the following:

◆ Do you feel that you're receiving enough delegated assignments?

◆ Do you feel that you're getting too many?

◆ How would you feel about getting some more responsibilities or doing some more projects?

◆ Are there some areas that particularly interest you that you want to grow in?

It's also a good time to discuss your observations about the following:

◆ How well the employee seems to be able to balance delegated work with his or her routine responsibilities

◆ Any evidence of interpersonal problems when the employee works with new people on delegated tasks

◆ How the employee's results with delegated tasks affect his or her overall appraisal; how delegation success could affect a promotion

◆ Your ideas for future assignments you'd like to delegate to the employee and how he or she could begin preparing for them

8

Chapter Summary

As you reach interim checkpoints in the delegation, recognize your delegatee's efforts, and at the successful completion of the project, reward the delegatee and celebrate your shared success.

Learning why the project ended as it did is extremely important so that in the future you can repeat your positive results and eliminate your negative ones. Therefore, at a debriefing with your delegatee, analyze what went right and wrong and decide how to improve future delegations. You may also want to get your boss's reactions to how you managed the delegation. Finally, you'll want to reflect on how you managed the whole process yourself so that you can become a better delegator with each assignment.

Performance appraisals give you an opportunity to step back and consider the cumulative effect of several delegations with your employees. Discuss with employees how they're developing, how they're contributing to the company's goals, how they feel about delegation and their skills, and what the future looks like.

Self-Check: Chapter Eight Review

Answers to the following questions appear on page 119.

1. Why is it important to share the credit or the blame for the delegation's final results?

   _____

   _____

2. What is one of the most meaningful ways to recognize a delegatee's interim success?

   _____

3. When recognizing a delegatee's final results, what should you always consider when choosing a reward?

   _____

4. List two ways to respond when a delegation fails and when to use each.

   _____

   _____

5. What role can the performance appraisal play in the delegation process?

   _____

   _____

8

Answers to Selected Exercises

Chapter One

Chapter Review (page 17)

1. a. Abdicating responsibility for a task

2. False—Supervisors should give employees the freedom to approach delegated tasks in their own way.

3. c. Because of company policy, I can't provide employees with the information they need to effectively solve problems and make decisions.

4. True

5. The supervisor who delegated it

Chapter Two

Chapter Review (page 28)

1. a. Priority activities related to organizational goals
    b. Developing employees

2. b. Estimating the amount of time you spend on each job activity

3. Delegate when:
    ◆ The activity doesn't make the most of your abilities but does make the best of someone else's.
    ◆ The payoff is low.
    ◆ The job is repetitive.
    ◆ You have much more expertise than the activity needs.
    ◆ You need to develop your employees.

4. Never delegate when:
    ◆ You need to discipline an employee.
    ◆ You want to praise an employee.
    ◆ A situation is confidential.

5. False—Delegating enjoyable tasks shows employees you care about them and provides them with an opportunity to grow.

Chapter Three

Chapter Review (page 43)

1. b. People who match this personality type enjoy meeting the public, working in teams, making speeches, and persuading others.

   d. These people are more concerned with facts than with feelings. They are thorough, analytical, and meticulous.

   c. These people are helpful, patient, empathetic, and loyal to their fellow employees and to the organization. They are team players who strive to maintain good relationships.

   a. People who match this personality type enjoy working by themselves, pay careful attention to detail, and are capable of concentrating on individual tasks for long periods of time.

2. e. b and d

3. False—Always take your employees' schedules into consideration.

4. True

Chapter Four

Take a Moment (page 54)

1. Issue #4—The supervisor should have determined whether Bill had training on the program and arranged for some before he started the project.

2. Issue #7—The supervisor should have warned Julia that Shipping was resistant to change.

3. Issue #8—The supervisor and Sherm should have agreed on the level of authority he had to spend funds.

4. Issue #3—The supervisor should have checked on Huong Le's current workload.

115

5. Issue #9—The supervisor should have made sure that Jacob understood and could meet the deadline.

Chapter Review (page 56)

1. a. You'll both be clear about expectations.
   b. The delegatee will have all the information she or he needs to start out with confidence.
   c. You'll create a consistent method for delegating instead of a haphazard approach that yields unpredictable results.

2. To maintain your credibility.

3. So that the employee (or you in an emergency) can take corrective action if necessary.

4. To be sure the employee is making progress.

5. a. How complex the job is.
   b. How many people are involved.
   c. How experienced the delegatee is.

Chapter Five

Chapter Review (page 71)

1. One of the best ways to be sure you and your delegatee understand each other is to ask for <u>feedback</u> from your delegatee.

2. False—Never ignore signs that a delegatee is hesitant or confused. Instead, ask for feedback regarding the delegatee's concerns.

3. a. Confusion regarding the task.
   b. Lack of experience.
   c. Disagreement with the assignment.

4. It gives the delegator and the delegatee the chance to engage in further dialogue without forcing the delegatee to openly state, "I don't understand."

5. Level of authority

Chapter Six

Chapter Review (page 86)

1. As a delegator, you have to keep an eye not only on what your <u>delegatees</u> have promised to do but also on what <u>*you*</u> have promised to do.

2. A supervisor who provides too much support may inadvertently send the message that he or she doesn't trust the delegatee.

3. A supervisor who provides too little support may inadvertently send the message that he or she doesn't care about the assignment.

4. d. Introverted People-Oriented (clearly defined goals, roles, and expectations)

   b. Extroverted People-Oriented (freedom from detail)

   a. Introverted Task-Oriented (a reminder that process is as important as product)

   c. Extroverted Task-Oriented (autonomy and authority)

5. **Rung 1:** The employee informs the supervisor of a problem and waits until the supervisor solves it and tells him or her it's solved.

   Rung 2: the employee asks the supervisor how to solve a problem and then follows those directions.

6. **Rung 3:** The employee generates and analyzes alternatives for solving a problem and then suggests to the supervisor what should be done. The employee and the supervisor decide together whether this is the best alternative, and the employee takes action.

   Rung 4: The employee makes a decision and takes action and then informs the supervisor immediately of the action taken.

   Rung 5: The employee makes a decision and acts on his or her own and informs the supervisor routinely.

Chapter Seven

Chapter Review (page 98)

1. Your decision about whether to intervene when you see your delegatee headed for disaster should be based on two things:
   ◆ How much the delegatee will <u>learn</u> from making the mistake.
   ◆ How <u>costly</u> the mistake will be.

2. One way to help an employee build confidence is by <u>breaking</u> an assignment into smaller, easier <u>tasks</u> that can be <u>shared</u> with you or another employee.

3. Your work-averse employees can become competent, confident decision-makers if you <u>insist</u> that they actually <u>do</u> the job!

4. To get people to take risks, make their own decisions, and thus profit from the delegation experience, do two things:
   ◆ Always talk about the <u>results</u> you want, rather than the <u>method</u>.
   ◆ Think "<u>Ask</u>—don't tell."

5. To get a "squeaky wheel" to stop complaining and accept an assignment, reexplain why the task is <u>important</u> and how it can <u>benefit</u> the delegatee's career. As a last resort, point out the <u>consequences</u> for not accepting the assignment or for intentionally doing it <u>badly</u>.

6. To get a superior-acting delegatee to work better with coworkers, describe how others <u>perceive</u> him or her, and explain that <u>getting along</u> with people is as much a part of his or her job as completing tasks.

Chapter Eight

Take a Moment (page 107)

Situation 1—A
Situation 2—B
Situation 3—B
Situation 4—A

Chapter Review (page 113)

1. It's important in order to maintain faith and trust and to ensure that your delegatee will want to accept assignments in the future.

2. Your sincere "thank you."

3. The delegatee's personality.

4. If you believe the employee made a sincere effort to meet expectations, turn the experience into the best lesson you can. If you believe the employee was negligent, use your company's disciplinary steps to apply anything from a reprimand to a termination.

5. Performance appraisals give you an opportunity to consider the cumulative effect of several delegations with your employees.